Hallelujah

A Story of Cancer, Love, and Grace

Wendy Johansson

edited by
Rachel Small

WestBow
P R E S S
A DIVISION OF THOMAS NELSON

WestBow Press books may be ordered through booksellers or by contacting:

WestBow Press
A Division of Thomas Nelson
1663 Liberty Drive
Bloomington, IN 47403
www.westbowpress.com
1-(866) 928-1240

ISBN: 978-1-4497-9245-9 (sc)
ISBN: 978-1-4497-9246-6 (hc)
ISBN: 978-1-4497-9243-5 (e)

Library of Congress Control Number: 2013907113

Printed in the United States of America.

WestBow Press rev. date: 6/13/2013

For my Dad; for the Grace and Harmony
and Love with which you lived your life.

For my God; for the many gifts you give to all of us,
the Love and Care you have for each of us,
and the Grace you continually bestow upon us.

Contents

Chapter 1

Introduction

*The only story that God cannot use is
the one that is not shared.*

—Unknown

This is a story about my dad. This is a story about my family. This is a story about cancer. This is a story about love. But most of all, this is a story about God's Grace. Hallelujah. This is a story about my journey with my dad's cancer diagnosis. It is a story about blessing out of brokenness. I believe, as many do, that in every blessing there is a burden and in every burden, there is a blessing. My life is completely blessed but there are times when I think the burden of all that blessing just might take me down. Each blessing, whether it is in the form of a spouse, a baby or child, a job, an opportunity, a ministry, a relationship, or a home, comes with the work required to maintain it—both a blessing and a burden. And the challenging times we face are both burdens and blessings. As we walk through the fire, we can arrive at a new point in our spiritual journey, stronger and closer to God. A blessing.

I think many people will understand my story and relate to it in some way, especially people who have experienced illness or the death of a loved one. And especially people who have walked with cancer somewhere on their journey. And especially people who have some belief in a higher power. Tielhard De Jardin, a philosopher and Jesuit priest, once said, "We are not human beings having a spiritual experience. We are spiritual beings having a human experience."

People often ask why God allows bad things to happen to good people. I don't believe that God is hanging around deciding which bad thing to give to which good person next. I believe there are many variables in our grand universe. But fundamentally, I believe the difficult or so-called bad things that happen to us provide us with great opportunities to grow personally, grow in faith, and grow closer to God. Adversity and suffering give us the opportunity to build strength and grow spiritually. And I have often thought that God has more capacity to be with us in the valleys, although I must admit I really do like the mountaintops.

Perhaps God is more likely to be with us in the valleys because we are more likely to seek, turn to, or invite God to be with us during hard times. Then God can shine His light on us, around us, and through us for His glory or glorious joy. Or "glory-us" joy. Under the burden of adversity, God can bless us in many different ways. Carol Kent, in her book *Between a Rock and a Grace Place*, discusses how God gives us divine surprises and splashes of joy when we are walking with heavy burdens. Her words encourage us to hold on to hope because we always have choices. Sometimes that is difficult to remember when you are in the valley but in my case, with the burden I was under, God's blessing was easy to see and easy to feel. Hallelujah!

I always thought I might write a book, or books, at some point in my life. After university I was fond of saying that my back up plan was to write a book, go on Oprah, and become a wealthy best-selling author overnight. Too bad the Oprah Show has gone off the air. I had thought that if I did write a book, it would be about parenting, or marriage, or personal finance, or life coaching, or health, or diet and fitness, or my life as a soccer mom, or something like that. But God had other plans.

People plan, God laughs.

This is my story . . .

About Me
(Feel free to skip this part if you don't want the backstory)

I was born in Calgary, Alberta, Canada, in 1964, to Diana and John Bennett. I have two older brothers, Brian and Robert, and an older sister, Katherine. My parents, both born in Montreal, moved to Calgary in the early sixties, and bought a house a few years later, where they have lived ever since. It gave me an appreciation for roots and I was always glad I lived in a family that didn't move around all the time.

My family was fun—I loved them. And I liked them too. They weren't perfect, but I had a nice childhood. I took tap dance and guitar, played softball and basketball, took drama, choir, and performing arts, and did well in school. My parents were very musical and academically oriented. They were both university educated and I always seemed to know that I would go to university as well. I graduated in 1987 from the University of Calgary with a Bachelor of Commerce degree in business. During my third year of university, I became a fitness instructor so I wouldn't have to pay for a gym membership, and I currently still work part-time teaching fitness classes. It's hard to give up being paid to exercise, and besides that, it's really fun.

Growing up, I was an agnostic. Around the age of nineteen, I started to wonder about God a little more. My best friend, Grace, had a very strong faith and was on a quest to know God more fully. In my third year of university, I had some God experiences that helped me really begin to know the Lord. I began to develop my spiritual sense and my faith journey began.

After my undergraduate degree, I worked for a few years with IBM and then went back to university in 1989 to get a degree in counseling psychology. I graduated in 1993 with a Master of Science degree specializing in marriage and family. Between both degrees, I managed to take so many dance classes that I finished with a minor in dance.

Dance is a spiritual experience for me, as is singing and playing piano and guitar. Grace used to say I was going to church when I was going to dance class. I felt very connected to God through dance and music. Creative expression can definitely be a spiritual experience, as well as a human one.

In 1989, I signed up for a holistic health course for fitness instructors in Hawaii just before I went back to university to do my master's degree. One of the books we read in the course was about visualization. At that point in my life I really did not think I would get married or have children. I said to God, "Okay, if you have a man out there who I could be happily married to, then bring him on." A few times, over the course, I visualized a husband and life partner in a prayer to God. Michael and I started dating in 1990, less than a year later.

The only hitch: he was an atheist. I said to God, "Really? An atheist? Are you sure?" And God indicated that it would be alright and not to worry. Within the first few months of dating, Michael and I had some heated exchanges about God and Jesus. At that point I decided I wouldn't get drawn into these arguments if at all possible. I prayed a few times, here and there, that Michael would come to know God.

We met at the crisis center where we both volunteered. Michael was working on his Bachelor of Social Work degree. We were married in 1991 and had our first baby, Carina, in 1992 during reading week, while I was in graduate school and Michael was in his last semester of his BSW. Just as I finished my thesis, we had our second baby, David, in 1993. I had my thesis bound the week following his birth.

Michael was leading a treatment program for Aboriginal adolescents with addictions to solvents. He then began a post-treatment program travelling to many different aboriginal communities all across Canada, especially Northern Canada. Early on in his travels, he had some very powerful spiritual experiences and began to know God, the Creator. That was the beginning of his faith. I remember the first time he told me about some of his encounters with God, "You won't believe this!" he said. "You won't believe what happened!"

I replied, "I won't believe it? Me? Are you kidding? You're preaching to the choir now!" God was right, of course—it didn't matter that Michael was an atheist. Now he was a believer.

Up until Carina was born, I thought I would have a high-powered career, but I very quickly realized I was probably going to choose to stay at home with her for at least a few years. Michael and I had decided early on in our relationship that we would like to have three or four children, so as soon as I had the energy we had our third baby, Andrew, in 1996. Before we had Carina, I had thought that we should have three kids close together so that I could get back into the workforce more quickly. However, after baby number three, I realized that juggling a career with three young children would be very difficult. In fact, it wasn't very long before I couldn't imagine trying to work full time and keep the family running on the right track. I had no motivation to try to get my career going. I was tired! I had thought of starting a home-based business to possibly get the best of both worlds.

When Andrew was born, I decided to home-school Carina for Kindergarten and then grade one. While Carina was in grade one, I started my own business in dance-fitness classes. At the end of her grade one year, I asked Carina what her favorite part of the year had been and she told me that she liked going to the recreational center where I worked and taking activity and craft classes with the other kids. So I decided to put her in school the following year.

To say that it was a crazy time in my life is an understatement! I was working part-time as a fitness instructor, running a business as a dance-fitness instructor, raising three young children, and trying to keep the house running smoothly and in order. I eventually realized that running a home-based business really meant working full-time hours without the help and support of outside child care. In retrospect I think it would have been easier to hire a nanny or day-home provider and work a full-time job that paid well. Still, it was a good experience.

In September 1999, Michael and I began attending church with the kids. We had been thinking about trying to find one since 1994, when Michael started developing his faith. I had prayed for a church a few times but had never actually seriously looked for one. It was hard to find the time, never mind the energy, but that month a friend of mine invited us to her son's baptism at a United church. We really liked the church and it seemed like a great fit for our family, so we started to attend regularly.

In a sermon a few months later, one of the ministers spoke about how we can connect with God and the Sacred through creative arts. After the service, I told her that I had experienced that connection through my dance and music.

She said, "You dance? I've been praying for a dancer to come to the church."

"Yes, I dance," I replied. "And I've been praying for a church!" It was a lovely, divine moment and that is how I became involved with liturgical dance and the dance ministry in the church.

In 2000, during the May long weekend, I had an epiphany: I was burning out. I had begun the nineties running myself ragged and finished off the nineties running myself ragged and the "ragged" was definitely starting to take a toll. I realized that I needed to give up my dance-fitness business or I was going to start paying with my health. After much analysis and angst, I gave up the business, and over the next year or two, I slowly began to feel more normal again. I attended the women's retreat at our church and the theme was *Slowing the pace, Deepening the faith, and Discovering Grace.* Very relevant, to say the least. I developed a new personal policy: do not take on anything new unless you are willing to give up something else you are already doing.

By 2002, I was feeling pretty good again. All three of our kids were in school and my life seemed much closer to some sense of sane. Carina was ten years old and I realized she was half way to being twenty, and I knew the kids would grow up very quickly. Michael had been talking about having another baby since . . . well, since Andrew was born. We decided to go for the fourth and in 2003, Arianna was born. For some reason, I thought I could handle it. Ha ha . . .

I participated much less in the dance ministry as well as church in general. After all, I had my new policy—and church was one of the things we gave up. This was also the beginning of the soccer-mom chapter in my life which is another book in itself. All three of our older children began to play soccer more seriously, both indoor and outdoor, after Arianna was born. I believe we peaked in 2008 when our family schedule included ten to fifteen soccer events per week, nearly year round. Luckily, it is more reasonable now. Hallelujah!

Today, I am a wife and mother of four kids ranging in age from seven to nineteen and all living at home. This is my full-time occupation. I also have three part-time jobs in addition to trying to volunteer in the church. I work as a fitness instructor, I am the property manager of the two properties that Michael and I rent out and just recently, I have done a bit of individual accounting and finance consulting. It's still a balancing act—but not anything like it was a decade ago. Hallelujah.

So, one very full-time job (some could argue wife and mother is actually double full-time), three part-time jobs, and now . . . a book. I could write chapters or even volumes about what I have just summarized in the last few pages but enough about me.

Back to the main story. In 2010, my dad became ill . . .

<u>Favorite Dad Memory:</u> When I was three or four, all six of us were watching "Laugh-In" on the old Admiral black-and-white television with the twenty inch screen, in my parents' bedroom. My dad was lying in his spot on the left side of the bed, and I was small enough for him to hold on his chest and abdomen. I was curled up, held in his arms—I could hear him breathing, and I could hear his heart beating, and I felt safe and secure and loved.

Lesson: Love is powerful.

Chapter 2

Dad's Prostate Cancer Journey

There are many things you learn in the darkness
that you cannot learn in the light.

—Unknown

We could never learn to be brave and patient
if there were only joy in the world.

—Helen Keller

On August 15, 2010, my husband and kids and I went to my sister Katherine's house for dinner to celebrate my nephew Mark's birthday. When we arrived, Dad wasn't there, which was very unusual. Mom told us that he wasn't coming. He had gone to the hospital earlier that day due to issues with constipation. In the moment that I heard that, I felt like God told me, "This is going to be bad." It wasn't an audible voice that I heard. God has yet to speak to me with an audible voice. Perhaps one day—I look forward to that. The thought was quite strong and didn't seem to be my own. Some, including me, would say it was the voice of the Holy Spirit.

And as the realization that this might be bad, began to sink in, I wanted to stand in a prayer circle and pray for my dad but I knew this might come off as a little too alarmist or extreme for my family. Constipation didn't seem like a serious issue but seemingly God had just told me that it was. So I sat through dinner feeling a little stunned. I had a flashback to more than two months earlier. My mom and I had travelled to Montreal together for my grandmother's funeral. When my uncle asked my mom, "How's John doing?" Mom replied, "He's not a well man." Her comment caught me off guard. I had had no idea that was the case, and I had had no idea then how right she was—perhaps neither had she. Dad had a history of heart issues but overall I had thought of him as being in pretty good health for a man seventy-six years old.

So at that dinner, stunned by my dad's absence, stunned by God's revelation, I started to try to prepare myself for what was to come—even though I had no idea how to do that and no idea of what was actually to come. That was the beginning of my dad's illness, at least for me. I knew God was with me and that I would not walk alone. Hallelujah!

Two days later, I called Dad and I was surprised by the sound of his voice—it was airy and weak. He sounded ill and disheartened and he told me he felt like he was sitting on a tennis ball. Dad's doctor had been monitoring his enlarged prostate or benign prostate hyperplasia (BPH) and his protein-specific antigen (PSA) was about nine or ten. Dad said this was not abnormally high for a man his age with an enlarged prostate. PSA is a marker for the presence of prostate cancer. Dad told me his doctor was not too concerned. *Maybe your doctor isn't worried*, I thought, *but I sure am.* I asked him if he was concerned that he might have cancer and he said he was. I told him I was too.

I was a little shaken up after speaking to Dad. *We have got to take action*, I thought. *We need to get things moving along and get Dad some medical attention and intervention!*

The next day I spoke to my brother Robert, who lived with Mom and Dad, and we both agreed that Dad needed medical help and that if we needed to get private health care or go to the United States then we should do so, whatever the cost. Neither of us wanted to waste time waiting in a queue. Dad had an appointment with his doctor that week and we hoped the process would get started.

The following weekend, Dad went back to emergency again for a bowel blockage. He was given three enemas and a laxative and sent home. Yikes!

His doctor arranged for him to see a urologist at the hospital two days later. On the morning of his appointment, Mom took him to the hospital emergency room. Finally, after fourteen hours of waiting, seeing doctors, a CT scan, a blood test, and an IV, Dad told them, "Either admit me or I am taking this IV out and going home." So they admitted John Bennett on August 25 at 1:00 a.m. I was glad that Dad was in the hospital because he would have more access to doctors, specialists, and procedures and would not have to get in the back of a line. Instead of being on a six-month or one-year waiting list, he could be at the front of the queue. The next line he jumped was the colonoscopy line which could have been up to a three-year wait.

The doctors said Dad had swollen lymph nodes. Also, one kidney was blocked but there was no sign of a kidney stone. He was on massive laxatives and oxygen as well. The writing was on the wall—I just didn't know it yet.

Robert said Dad looked like a ghost when he saw him on Friday evening (August 27). Due to a possible bowel infection, Dad wasn't being given any pain killers, despite being in kidney, rectal, and back pain with a sore throat and a tendency to gag due to a swollen uvula. The results of the colonoscopy were okay— apparently no colon cancer.

On Saturday, while Michael and I were driving out of town to attend a wedding, Michael received an email update on his

BlackBerry from Robert. It said, "No solid food and on clear liquids only. Dad is looking old." I cried. I was definitely worried.

The next day, Michael and I visited Dad for the first time. It felt like he had been in the hospital for at least a week but it had actually been only a few days. He didn't look too bad—in fact, he looked better than I'd thought he would. Dad said he wanted out of the hospital but was scheduled for a transurethral resection of the prostate (TURP) the next day—a procedure whereby material from the enlarged prostate is removed in order to treat BPH. Dad referred to it as being "reamed out." Yikes. He also said that they would be able to biopsy the prostate tissue, and that they were considering doing a liver biopsy and a bone scan. At the time, I didn't really comprehend what that meant. Much later, it made a great deal of sense. The doctors were trying to determine the extent of Dad's prostate cancer.

On Monday August 30, the TURP went well and the bone scan was done. Good news. But it didn't last.

We found out Tuesday afternoon that Dad had had a mild heart attack at three a.m. During the night, he had been taken to another hospital, where they performed an angioplasty, placed a stent in one of his blood vessels, and then brought him back to the cardiac care unit (CCU). It was right next door to ICU and was a very high-level care unit. In fact, I referred to it as the Cadillac care unit.

Our family was not given these details until after everything had been done. My mom and I were both disconcerted with the hospital staff's lack of communication. Michael recommended that we request a family meeting with the doctors. I later read that when a man is diagnosed with cancer, his risk of heart attack is ten times greater. As far as I knew though at that point, the doctors were only exploring the possibility of cancer.

Dad seemed to be doing okay—showing solid improvement in fact—and was waiting for a bed to open up on the cardiac unit. One of Dad's friends, a fellow singer from the men's Christian choir they sang in, brought him a copy of the CD they had just recorded, and a Discman. Dad really appreciated it as he had played an active role in creating the CD with the group's director. He had arranged one of the songs and named the CD.

I visited Dad again on Friday, September 3, while he was still in CCU. He seemed much better—even better than the first time I saw him in the hospital. He told me that his three doctors (cardiologist, urologist, and CCU physician) had stopped by earlier to tell him, "that he had cancer." It was official.

I took the news quite well—I think because I had already suspected it. He said he was still waiting for the biopsy results from the TURP. Then Dad asked me how I felt about the diagnosis. It was just like him to worry about me. I told him, "We all have cancer cells in our bodies—it is a matter of degree. I guess we have to wait and see how advanced it is."

Looking back, my response seems to reflect a bit of denial but I usually try not to worry about things until I have all the information. There is no point in trying to figure out how to cope before you have the whole picture. Then I asked him the same question. He essentially dodged it. I was concerned about how my mom would take it.

My aunt reminded us a few days later that prostate cancer can be a less serious form of cancer. Many men live several years with prostate cancer and the survival rate is high compared to that of many other types of cancers. It is estimated that 80 percent of men who reach the age of eighty have prostate cancer. Similarly, I have heard that a woman who lives to age eighty or older has some degree of breast cancer.

Over the weekend, Dad's bowel blockage began again. My mom called me Sunday morning to let me know that his condition had worsened. Michael and the kids and I were meeting Michael's parents for brunch, and on our way, we quickly stopped by the hospital to see how Dad was doing. He was in a lot of pain but the nurses were unwilling to give him pain medication since they thought it would make the bowel issue worse. I insisted—poor

Dad was in complete misery. While at brunch, I called Katherine, Robert, and Brian to update them while we tried to figure out what was happening and how to get Dad more pain medication and medical intervention.

That afternoon, Dad got to see the gastroenterologist (GI), who took x-rays of the stomach and did a sigmoidoscopy, both of which showed nothing. Dad was put on morphine and more laxatives. The doctor seemed to believe that it was paralytic ileus which is a pseudo-obstruction of the bowel—when the bowel appears to be obstructed but is actually impaired due to nerve or muscle problems that negatively affect the movement of the intestines.

When I Googled paralytic ileus, I found sixteen different causes on the website I checked, and two of them were kidney issues and tumors. I didn't connect the dots at the time but I didn't really have a context yet. I'm not sure if the doctors recognized the causes, but if they did, they did not communicate this to me or my family. I now wonder if the GI even consulted or communicated with the urologist or cardiologist. It certainly didn't seem like it.

Over the course of the week, Dad was moved to another ward and seemed to improve again, even though the bowel was still not functioning normally. On Friday, September 10, while I was visiting, his urologist stopped by to let him know the results of the prostate biopsy. Dad's PSA was low, between eleven and thirteen, and his Gleason score was ten. The doctor explained that usually the PSA would be much higher with that Gleason score—even in the hundreds or thousands. I had Googled prostate cancer that morning before going to the hospital, so I did have some idea that a score of ten was not good. I didn't get the full impact of that information until later, but I believe Dad understood it in that moment. I was fairly certain that he had researched prostate cancer before.

We also found out that the bone scan was "inconclusive, although suspicious." The urologist was fairly casual in his approach and did not make a big deal about Dad's case. He gave us the data but drew no conclusions. He suggested hormone therapy would be the main treatment approach. At the time I didn't realize what we had just been told, or moreover, what had been implied and not told.

Carina and I had to leave to pick up Arianna from school and regrettably, I didn't have time to stay and discuss any of it with my dad. In retrospect, I wish I had stayed because I realized later that my dad had just been told that he had advanced prostate cancer and that he was one of those rare cases where the PSA score does not accurately reflect the state of the advanced cancer in his body as it was supposed to do. Very unfortunate. Extremely unfortunate.

Later that afternoon I Googled Gleason score and then fully remembered what I had read earlier that day. The Gleason score is an indicator of the severity of prostate cancer, according to the tissue in the biopsy. The strength of the two strongest patterns of cancer cells are rated from one to five, five being the most aggressive or advanced, and then added together. Therefore, ten is the worst prognosis. What a horrible realization. Now understanding that we were up against something extremely serious, I went on the public library website and started looking for books on prostate cancer. I put holds on at least ten books, determined to find out much more about the disease.

Earlier that day, Dad had told me he had asked his cardiologist if he could be discharged. The cardiologist had said he was okay with that if the urologist agreed. Dad then told the urologist he was likely being discharged the next day as he had discussed it with his cardiologist. The urologist looked surprised but said okay. I think Dad had a plan to be discharged on Saturday and he told each doctor that the other was okay with it—a very clever ploy to finally 'breakout' of the hospital. He reminded me of a kid asking his parents for something by first telling Mom that Dad's okay with it, and then telling Dad that Mom's okay with it. Classic. He was discharged the next day. I now think that Dad finagled his way out of the hospital to go home to die.

Weeks later, I wondered about the way the urologist had told my dad about his PSA and Gleason score without clearly stating what the state of the cancer was. I wondered why we had not been sat down, ideally as a whole family, and told the news with a chance to process the information and ask questions and figure out what was happening. That little drop by visit from the urologist was very casual and very cryptic and of hardly any use at all.

And later on, I wondered why that had not happened on August 25 as well.

Favorite Dad Memory: When I was thirteen or fourteen, I thought it would be fun to learn a few barbershop songs and sing them as a family. Both Mom and Dad were very involved with Barbershoppers and Sweet Adelines— choruses and quartets. We ended up learning one or two tags (a barbershop tag is the last line of a song) and two songs. I thought we sounded okay. Dad referred to us as the "Family von Crap singers." I think it was a joke . . . perhaps. Dad had a way of looking at things objectively and critically, but he also had a great sense of humor!

Lesson: Don't take yourself too seriously.

Chapter 3

Escape From the Hospital

Maybe who we are isn't so much about
what we do, but rather what we're capable
of when we least expect it.

—Jodi Picoult, *My Sister's Keeper*

Saturday, September 11, Dad was discharged in the late afternoon and finally made it home. The next day I spoke to Mom and she was very worried. Dad was in bad spirits and very uncooperative. He had always been difficult when he was sick, and he really did make a crummy patient. And now he was Mom's crummy patient. The diarrhea was more severe and Mom became even more worried. I was concerned that Dad had possibly contracted a C-diff infection from the hospital, or had a perforated bowel, or was at risk of severe dehydration.

Now that I was reading about cancer and had started making notes, I tried to advise Mom on Dad's diet and suggest other things that might be helpful but I realized it would be hard to implement changes. It is challenging for any of us to make small changes over time, never mind major changes overnight. Also, Dad was not really interested and did not seem motivated to try anything, and Mom was just trying her best to cope with her own emotions, as well as Dad.

On Thursday, September 16, Mom, Robert, and I took Dad to his appointment with his urologist to begin hormone treatment (typically the only therapy offered for advanced stage prostate cancer). Dad seemed to look a little jaundiced under the fluorescent lights, and I wondered if his liver was functioning properly. We also wanted to address the issue of the diarrhea and possible infection. The doctor gave us a requisition for a stool test for C-diff and said he would look into the colonoscopy results. He didn't think the bowel issue was related to the prostate cancer.

I had a lot of questions now that I had done a bit of research. I wanted to know what stage of cancer Dad had and if it had metastasized and to where. I wanted to know where the bone scan looked suspicious since it was inconclusive, and how likely it was that the cancer had spread to those places. I wanted copies of all test results and a referral to an oncologist. I wanted to know the anticipated success of the hormone therapy given Dad's numerous health issues, and how and when it would be measured. I wanted to know if homeopathic options (vitamin D, omega-3s, greens plus, phytochemicals, bioflavonoids, melatonin, probiotics, etc.) would be compatible or useful as well as the impact of dietary considerations (such as low sugar, low dairy, low animal protein, macrobiotics). I wanted to know the real prognosis, as much as anyone could "know" it. I also didn't want to upset my dad or push the boundaries of his privacy. He had always been such a private man with respect to his health. In retrospect, it seems ridiculous considering what we were up against.

I came away with a little more information and no referral. The doctor did confirm what I had suspected: Dad had advanced stage prostate cancer and from my point of view, it didn't look good, despite the optimistic, cavalier, yet somehow aloof attitude of the urologist. If his goal was to be gentle and not shock or alarm anybody, he succeeded. I was bewildered that we had gone from constipation to stage four cancer in just three or four weeks!

I had read that the prognosis of an advanced stage prostate cancer patient was six months to five years. It seemed six months was more likely in my dad's case, but the fact that sometimes advanced stage prostate cancer patients survived for five more years after the diagnosis was encouraging. The urologist didn't offer up a timeline for Dad and I hadn't found the courage to ask.

The next day, I spoke to my friend Elena on the phone and I told her about my dad. She was so compassionate, and being a practicing yoga student-teacher, from a Hindu background, she asked me, "Would you like me to put him in the light?" I had never been asked that question before, and I was so touched. *Heck, yes,* I thought and I told her, "That would be wonderful!" Elena said she would put my dad in the light and devote her practice to him. She also wrote out a healing mantra for me, and gave me a mandala, which is similar to a rosary. Grace gave me a wooden rosary with a cross she had purchased in Jerusalem. I greatly appreciated the offers of support and prayer through that time. Friends are so precious when you are facing adversity. I was reminded of a quote from the film *Starman* (1984): "You (humans) are at your very best when things are at their worst."

On Saturday, September 18, I talked to Mom in the morning. Dad's feet were badly swollen, his appetite was declining, and he wasn't doing well. I Googled "swollen feet" and realized that it could be many things, two of which were liver failure and kidney failure. Unnerving and alarming.

I went over to their house that night since both Mom and Robert were going out and we thought somebody should stay with Dad and help with anything he needed.

"I guess you're the babysitter," Dad said.

"I prefer to call it dad-sitting," I replied. It was nice to be with him, just the two of us, but to see how poorly he was doing was hard. He seemed very sad, perhaps even depressed, and he was still in quite a bit of pain since he was only taking regular Tylenol. I had a few suggestions but Dad was only interested in two of them: melatonin and probiotics. He seemed only interested in what could help him with the problem of the moment—the melatonin could help him sleep and the probiotics might help his digestion. Dad was still eating three small meals a day, having trouble sleeping, and he easily tired if he got up to walk or go upstairs.

While discussing his pain, I found out he had a sore lower back and that he had seen a massage therapist on August 14, the day before he went to the hospital for the first time. It dawned on me that the soreness was probably due to cancer cells that had metastasized to the bone. A sinking feeling descended again.

Dad told me he wasn't sure what to pray for: a quick healing or a quick death. I very matter-of-factly but thoughtfully said, "Well, if it were me, I would pray for a quick healing and perhaps you could ask God if that is not an option then you could pray for a quick death—a sort of if/then approach." He seemed to like that idea. Now who was being cavalier about cancer and death?

I later read that due to PSA screening, less than 7 percent of prostate cancer diagnoses in the United States are stage four advanced cancers and one of the symptoms can be bone pain. Dad was part of that 7 percent. How completely unfortunate! I still don't know what Dad's PSA level had been in the months leading up to August 2010. I don't know how often or when he had been tested. I looked through his medical file he kept at home hoping to find some information about his PSA history but could not find any lab results. My family doctor informed me recently that a PSA of five or higher is a cause for concern and should be flagged. I think Dad must have ignored many symptoms. However, I was surprised his doctor had not been more proactive, although he had referred him to a urologist a few months prior but Dad was not able to get an appointment until September.

On Wednesday, September 22, Dad had an appointment with his family doctor in the afternoon, once again with the four of us.

Robert had noticed blood in Dad's sputum, and he was coughing up bile. Things seemed to be going from bad to worse. He was no longer able to walk on his own. Katherine had visited Dad on Monday evening and later said to me, "He should be in the hospital—anyone who looks at him would think he should be in the hospital!" I spoke to Katherine and Michael before I left to pick up Dad for the appointment. We all agreed: we didn't want to find out what was wrong with Dad at the autopsy. Ironically, we had the diagnosis, just no one to tie it all together for us.

For Dad's family doctor, Robert wrote a summarized history of Dad's issues since August 22. At the end of it, he wrote:

> *It is rather difficult to call or get a hold of anyone to advise us on what to do. Given that there are multiple medical problems (heart, lungs, prostate, bowel, kidneys, and liver) no one doctor seems to grasp the whole picture although the urologist is the closest.*

We were somewhat lost.

I had many questions for the family doctor. I wanted to know the history of Dad's PSA and BPH—year-over-year changes and when it first became elevated. I wanted to know if there was any information on the size of the prostate, measured in cc's, and if PCA-3 had been measured. I wanted a better pain medication for Dad, preferably tramadol or Tramacet, which are supposed to be effective with cancer and not as immunosuppressive as morphine. I also wanted him to have oxygen and an oxygen saturation meter, since cancer thrives in low oxygen environments. I wanted to ask about the flank pain Dad was having and his swollen feet—was that his kidneys, liver, dehydration, side effect of the hormone treatment or other medications Dad was on? I wanted to know how aggressive the cancer was and whether we could be referred to an oncologist, since prostate cancer is nearly always treated by urologists. I wanted to know if we could be referred to a geriatrician. I wanted to know if there was such a thing as a geriatric oncologist. I wanted to know what paperwork and test results the doctor had and his interpretation of them, since the paperwork we had been given had very little information.

We did get the tramadol and the doctor told Dad that if he got any worse, he should go to the hospital. There wasn't time to get many of my questions answered, despite the fact that we were in the examining room with the doctor for at least thirty minutes. For doctors in Alberta, this is a very long appointment.

We got Dad home again and sat down to talk.

"I want to go to a hospice and be medicated," Dad said.

"I understand," I replied, taken a bit by surprise. "You seem to have no will to fight, and no will to live," I continued. "Essentially, you seem like you have no hope."

"Yes," he agreed.

"I know you know that without hope, it may be impossible to improve," I ventured.

"I know," Dad said quietly—another profound, heart-wrenching moment on the cancer journey.

The strange thing was that I didn't really register that Dad said he wanted to go to a hospice. I seemed to be stuck in the reality of his hopelessness.

As I read more about cancer, I came across information about the Krebs cycle. I learned that cancer grows by getting as much sugar as it can and then uses the body's own energy cycle against it. When the cancer can really capitalize on this cycle, it robs the muscles and tissues of sugar and energy resulting in the buildup of lactic acid which causes muscle soreness. Eventually, cachexia, muscle wasting, takes hold. The cancer feeds itself and the body has to burn its own tissues for energy.

As I thought about this process, I had an "aha moment." I remembered last winter Dad had said on a few occasions: "My whole body aches, especially my legs." I had presumed it was the cholesterol medication he was taking, and I suggested he go off it to see if it helped. In hindsight, I realize that it was probably the cancer growing and spreading and Dad feeling the lactic acid buildup. This was a warning sign I wish Dad, his doctor, and the family hadn't missed. I don't know if he ever discussed it with his family doctor.

I have very few memories of praying to God to heal my Dad during that time. I know that I did pray for healing, strength, and guidance for my Dad, myself, and my family, but I don't have any memory of being in prayer which strikes me as very odd. I was so busy trying to figure out what was happening medically—reading books, researching on the Internet, writing notes—and looking for solutions, I wasn't very spiritually focused, which surprises me. Still, I seemed to know God was with me as I tried to figure it all out. Even as I sat in Mom and Dad's house while my Dad told me he had no hope, I didn't pray or cry out to God or say something to him about God or faith. I just seemed to be there, somewhat in shock, somewhat numb, not knowing what to do—still trying to figure out what was happening with my dad and his cancer.

Favorite Dad Memory: When I was twenty years old, I broke up with my boyfriend of over four years. A few days after, Dad invited me to meet him for a drink after work. This had never happened before. I realized after the fact that Dad really just wanted a chance to talk to me and make sure I was okay. During our conversation I told Dad how I was really starting to feel God and wanted to pursue my faith. Dad apologized and said he regretted not raising me to know God and not taking us to church more frequently. I told him not to be sorry and that I felt free to explore God and my beliefs and develop my relationship with God without being encumbered by church doctrine or other people's beliefs. I told him he had given me a gift. I knew that he and Mom had always believed in God, but they never pushed their beliefs on us in any way.

Lesson: Sometimes you show people the way by giving them room to grow and find their own way.

Chapter 4

Decisions, Decisions

I was never crippled until I lost hope.

—Nick Vujicic

Thursday, September 23 is a day that will be etched in my memory for a long time to come. Of all the difficult days we faced, this was one of the top three. With everything going on, I hadn't slept well the night before. Around mid-morning, Robert called—he had slept poorly as well. Mom too. Robert told me that Dad had slept well and the tramadol seemed to be working well. But, for the first time, Dad had stayed in bed that morning and did not want to eat, so Robert was worried. Dad had been completely exhausted the night before, and it had taken Robert one and a half hours to get him ready for bed. "It's almost more than I can handle," he said. "I'm hooped."

Robert wanted to call an ambulance to take Dad back to the hospital. He asked if I could come over to their house as he wanted my mom and the two of us to agree on this decision and convince Dad. I was not sure what to do, but I had been leaning towards taking Dad back to the hospital, since he seemed to be getting worse. I knew Dad did not want to go back. I knew this was going to be a tough decision. An impossible decision. An insane decision.

I arrived at Mom and Dad's house, and oddly, Dad looked pretty good. It seemed the new pain medication was working. He looked better and he said that he had slept well. To say that he definitely did not want to go back to the hospital would be an understatement. We discussed it.

"So what you're telling me is you all had a bad night and even though I had a good night, you want me to go back to the hospital?" Dad asked.

I laughed. Yes, that was one way to summarize it—smart of him. However, we had a feeling that something was not right and he was getting worse. Dad tried to convince us to wait one more night to see if he would turn the corner. He even started eating once the possibility of the hospital was on the negotiation table. In fact, he ate more for breakfast than he had all of the previous day. I think he just wanted to prove to us that he was okay and dissuade us from returning him to the hospital.

We decided to get some other opinions. I was able to get in touch with the family doctor within an hour, and the urologist returned my call from the day before. Speaking to both doctors on the phone within an hour could be considered a miracle in itself. They both recommended taking Dad to the hospital. We also called Health Link, a fantastic service—a group of nurses in a call center that provide a wide array of medical information. The nurse completed her assessment and told me, "Go to the hospital, just in case. If it were my dad, I would take him to the hospital."

How do you force a man like my dad, John Bennett, to do something you know he absolutely does not want to do? How do you take someone you love and respect and who has always been in authority over you to the hospital when you know he would almost rather die than go back to the place he so cleverly escaped from less than two weeks ago? I guess the question I had to answer at the time was would he *almost* rather die or would he actually rather die. I told Dad that the doctors and health link nurse recommended going to the hospital. After all our persuading and many discussions, Dad finally just stopped talking and arguing, and closed his eyes. I decided to take that as some kind of compliance. We dialed 911 and asked for an ambulance.

The paramedics came, assessed what they needed to do, and told us their plan. They called two firefighters to assist, since they couldn't use a gurney on the staircase. We watched two firemen and two EMTs carry Dad down the stairs and out the front door to the ambulance in a blue plastic hammock that looked like a small tarpaulin—like a sling. It was a crushing, despondent moment—a defining moment. My mom stood by, watching helplessly, looking sad and slightly desperate. She said to me, barely audible, "Wend, are you sure we're doing the right thing?"

Heck no, I thought, *I'm not sure, but it's too late to turn back now.* I answered, "I don't know—I hope so!" I hoped I wouldn't regret our decision later.

The EMTs took Dad out to the ambulance and started an IV to combat the dehydration. It seemed to be taking a long time, but we knew Dad's veins could be hard to find. While we were standing outside, deciding how we would get to the hospital, a neighbor of Mom and Dad's, and the father of a dear friend of mine since the age of three, came over to see if we were okay and if there was anything he could do. We told Matthew what was happening and he stood with us, offering words of support. As he was about to leave, I asked him if he would pray for Dad, knowing that our neighbor had a strong heart for God.

"Would you like to pray together now?" Matthew asked. My heart leapt in appreciation but I looked to my mom to see what she wanted, and she said yes, nearly crying. So Mom, Robert, our dear neighbor, and I stood on the front lawn encircled in arms, praying together. In all of the years we had lived on that street, I could never have imagined such a scene. I was grateful for the prayers and grateful for neighbors and friends with caring hearts.

Looking back, standing arm in arm in a prayer circle seemed natural with Dad being treated in the ambulance outside my mom and dad's house even though it wouldn't have seemed so natural on August 15, at my sister's house. It is interesting to note that we all have a threshold in a downward spiral where we can absolutely turn to God and lose the normal awareness we have of living in the secular world. It is different for everyone, but I believe nearly all of us turn to God at some point in a difficult crisis or life-and-death situation, perhaps for some even as we are dying. *Touched by An Angel* is a television show which aired from 1995 to 2003, about several angels who are assigned to help humans know that God loves them. I really enjoyed this show while it aired and always felt spiritually uplifted after watching it. There was a quote on an episode of *Touched by An Angel* by the angel Sam: "I've met a lot of men who don't believe in angels, but I've never met one who didn't want to." Happily, God is always there waiting, ready to seek us, as we seek Him. It is as if God is standing behind us and when we turn to look for Him, He is just there waiting and hoping we will turn around and see Him.

One of the EMTs finally came out of the back of the ambulance and told us they were ready to go to the hospital now. He said it had been very difficult to find a vein and as I studied his face a little more closely, he looked a little pale and somewhat shaken.

Once at the hospital, we walked through the standard process: waiting, registering, waiting, moving rooms, waiting, questions, nurses, waiting, examinations, tests, waiting. And all the while I was moving as though I was underwater holding my breath. The doctor finally told us the news. Dad was in renal failure and his kidneys were operating at less than five per cent.

The cancer had caused such swelling of the lymph nodes that both kidneys were blocked. If we had left him another day we most likely would have lost him—Dad would have likely died within twenty-four to forty-eight hours. It sounds crazy but I hoped I had not robbed Dad of the quick death that he had been praying for. Had we given him the one more night to turn the corner as Dad had pleaded for, he most likely would have died at home. And maybe that was the corner Dad wanted to turn.

Robert said to us, "Now I know for a fact that we did the right thing!" I wish I could have been so sure. I knew it was the right decision for us—if we had decided not to bring Dad to the hospital and he had died that night, Mom, Robert, and I would have had to live with the terrible guilt of knowing we could have taken him to the hospital and didn't. That would have been difficult for us for sure, but would it have been better for Dad? I didn't know the answer to that question.

One of the resident doctors did a very thorough examination of Dad and he concluded that the bowel issues were a result of the cancer. We left Dad in the emergency room at close to ten o'clock that night, sleeping. He looked much worse than he had that morning when he didn't want to get out of bed.

I went back to the hospital at ten o'clock the next morning, on September 24. They had a hospital bed on a cardiac ward open and were planning to move him. Dad was asleep. He looked terrible. I cried. I wasn't sure if I was going to be able to keep it together. The nurse said it had been touch and go through the night. His potassium levels were dangerously high. She also told me that the general internist wanted to hold a family meeting. I started calling everyone and setting it up. When my mom answered and I heard her voice, I started crying again—not a good idea since Mom would then think the worst. I quickly reassured her that Dad was okay—I was just a bit emotionally raw and overwrought.

Sometime in the past week I had learned that the first day Dad went to the hospital on August 25th, a CT scan had been done and the ER doctor had told my Dad while my brother Brian was with him that he had prostate cancer but Dad asked Brian not to say anything to the rest of the family.

At the family meeting that afternoon, the doctor talked about the kidney failure and Dad's creatinine levels being over 1500 umol(micromole)/litre. The normal range for an adult male is 60–110 umol/L. Serum creatinine is a waste product made from the breakdown of normal muscle and dietary protein intake. Healthy kidneys remove the creatinine and a high level means that the kidneys are not working to filter waste products from the body. She said they wanted to do a nephroscopy and a nephrostomy to insert tubes to drain the kidneys. She said that if it was successful and the creatinine levels decreased to below 300, then Dad would most likely avoid going on dialysis.

The doctor discussed the cancer and how it had spread to the lymph nodes and liver, they believed. We discussed Dad's living will and level of care. There is a hierarchy of designations to choose from depending on the level of intervention you desire: Resuscitation (R1, R2, R3), Medical (M1, M2), and Comfort (C1, C2). We chose R3, meaning if Dad required resuscitation, he would not receive CPR or be put on a ventilator.

This was the first doctor that I liked, the first doctor that communicated very well, and the first doctor that seemed to be able to be straight with us. Unfortunately, she was at the end of her six week rotation and another internist would be taking her place in two days.

Now as I write this, having reread all the notes and emails, I wonder how I missed the evidence of Dad's case myself, even though I am not a physician. It seems obvious in hindsight when you piece all the bits of information together:

Realizing that Dad and I had discussed the possibility of prostate cancer over the phone before Dad went into the hospital in August.

Realizing that the kidney issue surfaced the first week Dad was in the hospital.

Realizing that a conclusive CT scan had been done the first day in the ER that each physician understood to be advanced stage cancer without question (even though only Dad and my brother Brian knew this (for the first few weeks).

Realizing the paralytic ileus diagnosis of the bowel indicated a possible problem with the kidneys and/or tumors.

Realizing that swollen feet could be symptomatic of renal or liver failure.

Realizing that flank pain could be symptomatic of kidney issues.

Realizing Dad had a sore back and his appointment with a massage therapist on August 14, the day before this all started indicating the cancer may have metastasized to the bone.

Realizing that when a man is diagnosed with cancer, he has an increased risk of heart attack ten times that of normal.

Realizing that Dad had complained of generalized muscle soreness in the previous six to eight months.

Realizing that a common cause of death in prostate cancer cases is renal failure.

Realizing in emergency on September 23 that the bowel issue was related to the spread of the cancer—the resident doctor had informed us. (I later on had forgotten that fact).

Realizing that Dad had asked to go to Hospice the day before we took him back to the ER in an ambulance (also forgotten).

Of course, at the end, we had so much more information than at the beginning. And when you are going through such a turbulent, tumultuous experience, it is difficult to process what is happening moment to moment or even spend time reviewing previous events, conversations, notes, emails etc. I think this is a challenge for the doctors as well since their time is at a premium.

Surprisingly, none of the doctors ever succinctly pulled this information together for us in any kind of cohesive way. It would have been very helpful at the time, to have a doctor sit down with us and say: Your father/husband has advanced stage prostate cancer. The kidney issue is a result of the cancer metastases. The bowel issue has been diagnosed as paralytic ileus which we believe is a result of the impaired kidney function and cancer. Even though the bone scan is inconclusive, we strongly suspect the cancer has metastasized to the bone given the back pain. The heart attack may be a result of the cancer diagnosis and organ failures. And by the way, here is our prognosis and what you can expect with this stage of prostate cancer.

It would have been especially useful prior to Dad going into ninety-five percent renal failure. It would have been even better on August 25 when the definitive CT scan had been done. I don't know that it would have changed the outcome but it might have changed the process and helped us navigate more easily. I realize now that often it wasn't until I heard information two or three times that it began to sink in. I think doctors might want to keep that in mind when they are dealing with families directly as they were in our case.

It is sobering to realize now, after going through the many notes and emails, how much information was right there in front us—more than I realized at the time. I'm not sure if the doctors just didn't care that much because Dad's case was so serious and there was not time, if they felt helpless because they couldn't do that much for him, if it was a simple case of lack of resources and time, if there was a lack of a lead doctor in charge of the case, or if they were just incompetent. Or all of the above. Either way, sometimes their performance was not that impressive. There were too many doctors involved and no one leading. Too many cooks in the kitchen, so to speak. We never did get to see an oncologist.

I had read online that eighty percent of prostate cancer patients are treated by urologists. Dad would have only been referred to an oncologist if they wanted to give him chemotherapy or radiation treatment. But Dad's case was too far advanced for standard cancer treatment. It was a frustrating process.

That night Dad did eat and drink water but he was groggy and he wasn't strong enough to hold his own cup. His brother had flown in from Ontario to visit him, which at the time I was worried Dad would think he was dying as relatives from outside of town came to say goodbye. That seems insane or absurd now, considering he had told me he wanted to go to hospice two days before and he had been very close to dying. But I wanted to safeguard any shred of hope Dad might have.

We were on a wait and see plan over the weekend as the kidneys continued to drain and were hoping we would know more on Monday. On Saturday September 25, we could see Dad slowly improving and his creatinine levels had already declined to 1200 (300 down 900 to go). His kidneys appeared to be unblocked and the output was good, even though it was artificial via nephrostomy tubes. We realized the acid reflux, nausea, and swollen uvula in the prior week or two may have been due to the high creatinine levels. Where's Doctor House when you need him? His heart rate was elevated, in arrhythmia or tachycardia. The pain medication was delayed because they did not have tramadol on the ward. Apparently, laxatives were being given to expedite the potassium from his system so he was still being hydrated through the IV. He looked better than the day before and he could hold a cup so his strength had improved somewhat.

My husband Michael and I were attending a fundraising Gala that evening so we stopped by the hospital to visit, en route, dressed in our fancy party clothes, like Cinderella going to the ball. It highlighted a dichotomy that we had felt through the whole process: that feeling you have when you are in a crisis and yet you still carry on living your life as best you can and it feels like you are on two tracks. The normal track of your life and the crazy track of the crisis called cancer. My dad was lying in a hospital bed, nearly having died two days earlier, and I was off to a fundraiser to support my husband's career. In a crisis, it is amazing how much of your life you can let go of or postpone and it is also amazing how you can get through the more mundane tasks that you have to get through as well as the many tasks of the crisis such as hospital visiting, consulting, updating, phone calling, texting, emailing, conversing, Googling, reading and researching, praying, even worrying and crying. Hallelujah.

Carina, our eighteen year old daughter, had also come with us to the hospital. She had made a card for her granddaddy, to express her feelings and help cheer him up or give him hope. When he looked at it, he was very moved, and he teared up, as did I. It was a beautiful card, larger than life even. She made a picture collage using forty-five photographs on poster cardboard and wrote inside:

Dear Granddaddy,

> *I know you're in a lot of pain and you've suffered more than I can imagine. But I believe that you can make it through this with the help of all the people in your life that love you. You will never be alone.*
>
> *I've been praying for you, and I will keep praying. I love you ever so much and I couldn't ask for a better grandfather. Don't lose hope because I for sure will not, and keep fighting!*

> *Infinite amounts of love,*
> *Carina*

Carina managed to capture in photo and word what we all felt.

I helped Dad eat since he wasn't strong enough to feed himself and he seemed a little more cheerful by the time we left compared to when we arrived.

On Sunday September 26, we managed to arrange another family consult with the general internist. Dad was given a blood transfusion and his arrhythmia had subsided and blood pressure normalized. His creatinine levels were down to 900 umol/L—now 600 down, 600 to go. There was still some debate within the family about Dad's condition. Someone asked, "Are you sure it is advanced stage cancer?"

"Yes, the cancer is everywhere!" the good doctor replied. "Here, let me show you on this screen. Look at this CT Scan," she instructed.

"When was this done?" I asked.

"August 25, by the ER doc." she replied.

That was the day Dad was admitted to the hospital, I thought to myself. So, there it was. The doctors knew the "cancer was everywhere" since Day One. I wished we had had that information then. I wished Dad and Brian had not kept that a secret. That certainly was the end of any further debate. I wondered if Dad had been told how advanced the cancer was in the ER that day.

The doctor said that it would be highly unlikely that Dad would go home and that he would need to stay in care. She also stated that there was some possibility that Dad could have a heart attack or some kind of failure although that was unlikely since he had had an angioplasty, a nephrostomy, and was on an IV in the hospital. I was trying to press her for more details but she was still somewhat elusive with me and she had to go to another meeting.

Dad had been in a lot of rectal pain the night before—a five on a pain rating scale of one to ten, which we had begun to understand was quite conservative, by this point. My brother Brian asked me, "Do you understand the John Bennett Scale of Pain?" Dad had never rated his pain beyond a six. So anything beyond a four was very serious. Someone commented, perhaps the internist, that maybe Dad was saving a rating of pain beyond the level six for something very horrific. We needed to get him on a scheduled dosage for pain meds.

On Monday September 27, Mom and I wanted to tag team our visits in order to be at the hospital during the day to meet the new internist coming on for the next six week rotation but I had to leave after three o'clock and was unsuccessful. I had asked Dad if he would like to have a pain medication on his IV drip that he could control like he did when he was recovering from heart surgery years before. He said that was a good idea and it would be nice. I had wanted to discuss this possibility with the new internist but I didn't get the chance.

Early on, I had read that tramadol was a great pain medication for cancer patients for several reasons but the previous night I had read that tramadol is in the morphine family and is not good for people over the age of seventy-five and people with kidney or liver issues. So I no longer cared so much about how he got pain relief as long as he got it and I thought it would be much more effective if he could control it himself instead of relying on doctors, nurses, and family.

He was supposed to go for a chest x-ray but we were not sure why. I had bought a high powered liquid nutritional supplement as well as an immunity building supplement on the weekend but it was so strong in taste that it made me gag even though I was hoping Dad could take it. The other one was a fairly large pill so I wasn't sure if my dad would be able to swallow it since he had been having trouble with that and gagging with some of his oral medications. My hopes were dashed. Dad was not interested anyway.

The heavy duty laxatives were stopped now that Dad's potassium levels were normal but there was still concern about bowel blockage so an x-ray was planned. They also wanted an x-ray of the chest due to concern about gurgling in the lungs and a possible build up of fluid due to the IV which also was ceased in the hope that Dad could drink more fluids. Dad was able to shift in bed now and his creatinine levels were down to 600 (900 down, 300 to go). The nurses had put leg wraps on Dad in order to aid circulation since he was not getting out of bed and moving but they were uncomfortable and cumbersome.

That evening, my sister Katherine said that Dad was pulling himself up and flexing his legs. In fact, the nurse suggested he swing his legs over the side of the bed and Dad did so with support. The nurse asked him if he would like to sit in the chair and he said yes. So with support, Dad sat in a chair while the nurses changed the bedding, while Katherine and my brother Brian looked on in shock and surprise. Encouraging. Brian said he was quite surprised because after last Friday, he didn't think he would ever see him sitting up or out of bed again.

That same evening, I had been reading online about advanced stage cancer. I started reading descriptions of end-stage cancer and realized that could be my dad. I understood end-stage cancer to be the end of the advanced stage leading to death. Some of the descriptions fit with where Dad was at. Yet another loop to be thrown into. *Was this end-stage cancer,* I wondered? *Was Dad going to die very soon?*

On Tuesday September 28, I went to visit Dad, again with the hope of meeting the general internist. I did meet with him and five residents since I was lucky enough to be there when they were on their rounds. The doctor asked to speak to me in the hallway. The chest x-ray showed pneumonia on one lung. Dad also had a urinary tract infection which was not much of a surprise. Antibiotics would take care of both. The doctor didn't think Dad was competent enough to make decisions with regard to his level of intervention or care or with IV drip pain medication such as morphine. He was willing to put Dad on a regularly scheduled dose of pain meds. I think he was worried Dad would try to kill himself by overdosing if Dad was able to control his own medication level.

The doctor wanted to lower Dad's care level to M1 (Medical 1) and he said if something were to go wrong it would not seem prudent to send Dad to ICU. He said, "It would almost be unfair."

Again I wondered if it had been unfair to bring Dad back to the hospital last Thursday.

"Is this end-stage cancer?" I asked the internist, since that was what I had been concluding from the reading I had been doing the night before.

"Yes," he replied, "most definitely, end-stage cancer. We are talking days to weeks, not months. The cancer is everywhere." I had read that Stage IV prostate cancer patients can live anywhere from six months to five years. It did not look like we were going to get anywhere near that much time. "Does your mother know how bad it is?"

"I'm not sure but I think so," I replied.

"Are you and your siblings all on the same page?" he asked. I wasn't even sure I knew what page I was on. The pages kept turning too quickly to keep up.

"I'm not sure—maybe," I said. "If this is end-stage cancer, what do Dad's gains in strength over the last four days mean, then?"

"It's not really progress or recovery," the internist replied dismissively. "It's just because of the artificial kidney drainage due to the nephrostomy tubes." Wow!

I wanted a doctor to give it to me straight-up, but that was a lot to process even though I knew what he was saying sounded like the truth. I then began referring to this doctor as Dr. Doom. But I had to give him credit. He provided information and opinions and wasn't afraid to speak the truth as he saw it. Too bad we didn't have him on August 25.

Dad's spirits were very low that day and he wasn't interested in eating. He was difficult to speak with since he was not that responsive, replying with only one or a few words. While I was there, the nurse got him sitting in the chair. I knew I had to clarify some things with Dad since the doctor and I had spoken.

"Are you not eating because you are not hungry or because you don't want to prolong this?"

"Both," he answered.

"What is your level of suffering?" I asked. He looked thoughtful, then sad, then like he might cry, and didn't say anything in reply. I waited. Then I stated, "We need to figure out what level of care and intervention you need."

"Yes," Dad replied with a little more interest.

"What do you want?"

"Spirit."

"Pastoral Care?" I inquired.

"Maybe."

"Spiritual care?"

"Yes."

I waited for a while and then asked, "What spiritual care?" He did not say anything in reply. I asked again.

"I don't have a drinking problem," Dad said. Hmmm. So then I wasn't sure how lucid Dad was but it was the only answer to my questions that didn't seem to make sense.

"What do you want?" I tried again.

"Go to sleep," he answered.

"And be done?" I clarified, slightly desperate.

"Yes," Dad confirmed. *Wow.* Staggering. Chilling.

"Dad, I'm sorry if I took away your chance for a quick death last week," I apologized, crying.

"Don't worry about it," he said.

"Can you forgive me?" I asked sadly.

"Don't feel guilty," Dad replied. *If only it were that easy,* I thought.

"Do you want to go to Hospice?" I continued. He looked thoughtful but didn't say yes or no but he perked up quite a bit as if the conversation seemed to interest him. "I will try to get you whatever you want," I promised him. He didn't have any ideas or requests.

My brothers and sister and I decided to meet at my house that night. Clearly we needed to discuss what had been said by the doctor, as well as by Dad. We decided we agreed with a decision to move his care level down to M1, if that's what Mom wanted. In hindsight that was probably not the best choice. There did seem to be a definite shift in how the medical staff treated Dad based on his care level designation. It's as if you stamp, *On His Way Out* on the forehead versus, *Down But Not Out Yet.*

We looked at Dad's Personal Directive and decided we needed to make sure we were clear about what Dad wanted but we wondered if we could establish what he wanted. We wanted to be clear about his condition. We also decided to look into palliative care and exactly what options they might offer. We wanted to make sure we minimized the pain Dad was in and we wanted to try our best to find out if there was anything we could do for him with regard to visitors or ministers and chaplains.

I was stuck by one phrase from Dad's personal directive: If my condition is unclear, I would like to be treated by my caregivers to the best of their ability until my condition is known. In retrospect, Dad's condition should have been clear and yet somehow it never seemed to be. Every time we thought we had a handle on it, it seemed to change. It seems crystal clear in hindsight, as I write this, but it certainly wasn't at the time.

The next day my brother Brian sent out an email about an anti-cancer bracelet that he had been wearing. I clicked on the link and it turned out to be a website for an integrated cancer care centre in Vancouver. They had a publication, called the *Integrative Cancer Care Guide.* It was fabulous! It was a very succinct guide to many of the complementary and homeopathic treatments I had read about. I called the clinic to see if I could get a consult over the phone but they would only treat patients who could physically get to the clinic. Disappointment.

I also noticed somewhere that the hospital Dad was in had a Mind/Body Clinic. I called to see if they offered any complementary or alternative therapies but they really didn't offer anything like that. More disappointment.

On Wednesday September 29, my husband Michael went up to the hospital on his way to work and spoke to the nurse assigned to Dad for the day shift. Michael said we would like to request a time with the internist to discuss Dad's case with us which was arranged for noon. My brother Robert wrote:

> *Today was hard. Dad openly refused his medication and said he wanted to die. He was quite aware of what he was saying and his wishes were in turn expressed to the Doctor. They are changing his status from R3 to M1 which simply means that in the event of something happening that is life threatening he will not be transferred to ICU but be allowed to pass away. The funny thing was, he is sitting up and has quite the hand grip. We said a prayer over him lead by Katherine. The general internist was quite candid and said the cancer was going to take him, maybe not today but soon. He suggested that Palliative Care be brought in and that is happening.*

Palliative care is defined by the World Health Organization (WHO) as "…an approach which improves the quality of life of patients and their families facing life-threatening illness, through the prevention, assessment and treatment of pain and other physical, psychosocial and spiritual problems." The problem with palliative care is that it can be equated with end-of-life care but it is much more than that. However, this distinction did create some conflict within the family and whether or not we needed palliative care.

The palliative care nurse visited Dad on Thursday September 30. It had only been a week since we had brought Dad back to the hospital even though it seemed much longer. My daughter Carina and I walked in part way through their visit. I emphasized the importance of pain management which we never seemed to be able to resolve satisfactorily. The palliative nurse and doctor put Dad on dilaudid, a morphine derivative, and decadron, a corticosteroid four to five times more potent than prednisone. I thought the visit was positive and it felt like palliative care could be helpful.

I wrote in an email update:

> *If there is any hope at all then I think this might be the ticket since Dad's will to live and spirit to fight is so completely depleted. The decadron may also be a shot in the arm and a boost to his spirits. I guess we will see. At this point I think if we can tell him everything we give him is for comfort and won't prolong his life, we can get his cooperation—if he believes anything he takes or does prolongs his life e.g. eating, then he isn't interested. Oddly, I have seen physical and cognitive improvement every day since last Friday—the day the nephrostomy tubes were inserted in his kidneys. On the weekend I definitely would have commit to end-stage cancer but every day since seems a little less so. We are trying to reconcile the duality of knowing he could pass away any minute with the shreds of hope coming from what seems like physical improvement. The last creatinine level I heard was 360 so he is nearly out of the woods with avoiding dialysis. Yesterday Dad seemed calm and quite lucid and in less pain and discomfort. So I am still praying for his healing and for no suffering . . . We'll see how it goes . . .*

I made a chart for the family to use to keep in Dad's room so that we could write each other notes and keep track ourselves how Dad was doing. I took the cover off my journal and glued it to a new notebook. I also made a chart to fill in information about Dad through the course of the day and left these in Dad's room.

On Friday October 1, I asked Brian if he had Muscle Milk to bring in for Dad. I thought that if we could increase his protein and caloric intake, it might impact the proteins in his blood and reduce the swelling in his legs. The doctors did not want to put Dad on Lasix (or furosemide) which could be used to reduce the swelling or edema. A friend had suggested it but the doctor said it would work against the kidneys. In the space of a little more than a month, our knowledge of Dad's condition had gone from a problem with constipation to end-stage cancer. Still, it seemed like any small solution or drug we could try might be helpful whether it was nutritional supplements or pharmaceuticals.

Dad seemed in better condition Friday morning although a little groggy, perhaps due to the new medications. He told me he saw water coming from the ceiling and recommended I go get someone to fix it. I told him I didn't see that and it might be just his imagination. That sounded better than telling him I thought he was hallucinating. That also may have been the new drugs.

Mom had been to her family doctor (the same one as Dad's) that morning and she told me that the doctor was unhappy that the internist said that Dad was in end-stage cancer and would likely die very soon. Their family doctor planned to stop by the next day to visit Dad in the hospital.

The internist and his residents stopped by and I found out Dad's creatinine level was down to 260—now below the required 300 mark. That was good news. He said they would leave the nephrostomy tubes in since it would not be worth internalizing them for only one to two weeks of life. However if Dad started getting up and walking, they would reconsider. Dad's lungs were showing signs of improvement and the antibiotics at this point were only precautionary. The nurses discussed the possibility of Dad moving to the palliative unit but there was not a bed available yet. The level of care had been changed from R3 down one rung to M1 so if anything started to go wrong, there would be no resuscitation, no CPR or AED (paddles). Things were looking both good and bad—more duality.

There was the duality of my life: keeping my home and family going on its day-to-day course while knowing my father's life was hanging in the balance and trying to do everything I could for him.

Then there was the duality of Dad's situation: was he going to bounce back, even a little bit, and get better for a while? Could he possibly get the six months that a stage IV prostate cancer patient might get? Was he going to die any minute?

It was hard to know which course of action to take, at every turn. Of course I wanted him to live, but not in prolonged suffering. I knew God could save him, but would God save him? Was that God's plan? *Should I be trying to save Dad in case God's plan was to save him*, I wondered. This seemed, at times, a delusional thought, and yet I didn't know what God's plan was. What did God mean on August 15th by "This is going to be bad?" Did God mean that Dad was going to die? Or almost die? Or did God mean it would be bad but we would get through it?

Who knew . . . I wish I had.

<u>Favorite Dad Memory:</u> When I was in grade three, I had a teacher named Miss Snyder. When Miss Snyder got angry with a student, she would stride angrily over to the chalkboard, write their name in the detention column, write a five beside it, then circle it, indicating a five-minute detention—all with an angry demeanor. If the same student misbehaved again, Miss Snyder would change the number to a ten and then a fifteen and so on. If she really became angry, she would stomp up to the student, grab him by the shoulders, and shake him. I found this quite intimidating and was afraid that she might grab me and shake me. If you knew me in grade three, you would laugh. I was probably the last student who would ever get her name written on the chalkboard, never mind grabbed and shaken.

I relayed this situation to my father at dinner one night and he casually said to me, "If she tries to grab you and shake you, kick her in the shins and run. Leave the school and come home. Your mother and I will deal with it." With that one simple answer, I felt empowered to defend and protect myself and knew that my dad and mom would defend and protect me. They had my back! I later realized what a profound moment that was.

Lesson: In a family, you have each other's backs.

Chapter 5

The Miracle Days

. . . the Lord; he turned to me and heard my cry. He lifted me out of the desolate pit, out of the mud and mire; he set my feet on a rock and gave me a firm place to stand. He put a new song in my mouth, a song of praise to our God. Many will see and revere and put their trust in the Lord.

—Psalm 40:1-3 (NIV)

Those who look to him are radiant;
their faces are never covered with shame.

—Psalm 34:5

The Song

On Thursday September 23, my mom, Robert and I had decided to take Dad back to the hospital even though Dad didn't want to go. It was a heart-wrenching decision since I was sure if he had been stronger, he would have refused to go. After we got Dad to emergency, and were told he was in kidney failure, the week that followed was very difficult because Dad really had no will to live or strength to fight as he had been hoping and praying, for either a healing or a quick death. It was so hard for him and for us, but especially for him. Three days later, on Monday September 27, I was driving home from the hospital and heard this song on the Shine FM radio station—a Christian music station. I started to cry, so I pulled over and just listened and cried.

"Hallelujah" by Heather Williams, Tim Williams and Jamie Moore

Jesus, please come; please come today.
Heal me, hear me, be near me I pray.
I have fallen so far, flat on my face.
I'm in need of Your Grace today.
I stumble and fall but in spite of it all,
Your love always stays the same.
Hallelujah. Hallelujah.
Jesus, please come; please come today.
Break me; mold me. Use me I pray.
But don't give up on me now.
I'm so close to You now.
I'm in need of Your Grace today.
Wipe the dirt off my face, hold me in Your embrace.
Your love always saves the day.
Hallelujah. Hallelujah.
On my knees here I fall, in spite of it all, hallelujah.
And though it seems hard, I'm still trusting You Lord.
Hallelujah. Hallelujah.
I have fallen so far, flat on my face.
I'm in need of your Grace, today.
Hallelujah. Hallelujah.
Sing Hallelujah, sing Hallelujah,
Sing Hallelujah, I pray.
Jesus, please come; please come today.

him to the palliative unit. Apparently Dad had told Brian the same thing. It was four days ago that Dad had told me he wanted to die and wanted palliative care. The day before, the palliative team had changed his pain medication and started him on a strong steroid. We wondered if he was hallucinating again since he had seen water running down the walls that morning. We all went into Dad's room and gathered around his bed.

Dad launched into a long speech, veritably a soliloquy, about what he thought might happen, how he could be wrong in his perceptions and how he wanted each of us to tell him what our perceptions were. He talked about the ceremony, the pill to stop his heart, and moving to the palliative unit. I was shocked—not as much by what he was saying but more to the fact that he was saying it. It was the most I had heard him speak in two weeks—cumulatively—by far! The previous week, he had spoken only one to three words at a time. I couldn't believe it. He looked totally calm, totally relaxed, and he was sitting up in his bed with his lower legs crossed in a way I hadn't seen in over two weeks. *Was this the steroid? Was it God? Or was it both?*

We responded to everything Dad said. I told him there was not a ceremony planned or a pill to take. I told him euthanasia is illegal in Canada (although not entirely since you can elect not to save somebody as well as stop feeding them by intubation if they aren't eating). I told him my perceptions of the past week and how I could see his physical body improving as his kidneys improved and his creatinine levels declined. I told him that despite his physical improvement, I could see that his emotional and spiritual state was declining since he had lost all hope and wanted to die. As I had been speaking, my sister Katherine and her husband Will had arrived and joined in the conversation.

"Diana, what do you think?" he asked my mom. "I would like to hear from you."

"I don't want you to die, I want you to live," she replied, crying.

It was truly an amazing moment and I couldn't believe the change. I thought to myself, *this feels like a miracle.* I looked over at Michael and mouthed the words, "It's a miracle!" After over an hour, or possibly two, of discussion (I'm not sure since time seemed to stand still while I was in *The Twilight Zone*), Dad pronounced, "Well, if you all have hope, then I will too." Hallelujah!

"Let's listen to my CD." Dad said. "Put on the Master's Singers CD and let's listen to the first track." Katherine put it on and we listened to *My Redeemer*—Dad closed his eyes, conducted with his hand a little, and soaked up the music. Then we listened to *All is Well with My Soul* and enjoyed the pure grace of that moment.

This was such a dramatic change from the day before and the previous week that I was shocked, stunned, astounded, electrified, mystified, delighted, but most of all, grateful. It started to become clear to me that Dad had become more of himself again, stronger, with a renewed sense of hope. His spirit had been healed or re-enlivened. It was a moment of true Grace and I could feel God's Grace in the room. At the time, I wasn't sure why this unexpected change had come and yet still I realized that God had touched my dad and was holding him in the palm of His hand. We had our father and husband back with us in a way we hadn't in weeks. Dad was back in the game with some hope and was willing to try. It was unbelievable . . . but despite that, I believed it! Hallelujah!

Later, I looked up the definition of Miracle:

1. a marvelous event manifesting a supernatural act of a divine agent;
2. an unexpected event attributed to a divine intervention;
3. an extraordinary event manifesting divine intervention in human affairs.

Well, this event was definitely marvelous, unexpected, and extraordinary, and it most definitely seemed Divine. But still, in the back of my mind, I wondered how much of this upswing in Dad's progress was due to the steroid decadron. Friends of mine told me that it is not uncommon for a patient to have a rally near the end of life when death is near. Was this Dad's rally? There seems to be some agreement amongst those who work with the dying that an upsurge of energy can occur the day before someone dies or even as much as a month before someone dies.

I wanted to be rational and not attribute meaning where it didn't belong. But even as I write this, looking back, there is no question in my mind about what my experience was—it was definitely an experience of divine intervention and God's Grace. I believed this—but I wondered, *Will anyone else?*

The next day, Saturday, October 2, Brian visited Dad in the hospital in the afternoon. He was the only immediate family member who hadn't been in Dad's room the night before. Afterwards, Brian wrote an email to all of us:

> *The change is truly extraordinary. A week ago I believed he would be gone in a matter of days. His physical health remains precarious but I know this, however it happened, his spirit has been healed. He has chosen life. Dad's comment to me was, "Whether I have two days or two years, I will enjoy what I can." The following quote reflects a portion of my feelings towards Dad as a father:*
>
> *"He didn't tell me how to live; he lived, and let me watch him do it."*
>
> —*Clarence Budington Kelland*
>
> *Something else extraordinary is happening. In the decisions he has made in these last few days, he is showing us the way again. In the midst of a hundred big and little hurts and indignities, we see humor and kindness and strength and will and grace. When our time comes, and it will, we can see a way for Dad will have walked down the road a bit and he is letting us watch him do it still.*

I still didn't know who sang this song that led up to this miracle on Friday October 1. On Sunday, Michael and I took Arianna to the park and as I watched her play, Michael tried to find the artist of the song on his BlackBerry. No luck. After we got home, we were getting ready to go out to dinner—it suddenly occurred to me (or did God nudge me?) that I should check the Shine FM website. I couldn't find the song in the playlist but when I clicked on, *What's Playing Now*, there it was, currently playing on the radio. Wow!

I called the radio station and left a message asking them if they could let me know the name of the song and the artist. Janelle, from Shine FM, called me back the next morning and left me a message—it was called, *Hallelujah* by Heather Williams. In that moment I thought: *I've got to choreograph and dance to this song.* Even though I hadn't been very involved with the dance ministry in our church recently, I thought that this would be a great piece to keep in mind to choreograph and dance to at some point in the future.

I looked it up on You Tube and there it was.

In the video, there is a picture of a little girl with long brown hair that reminded me of how I looked as a child. At the end, there is a picture of a blonde girl that reminded me of my friend Grace when she was young, and a scripture that read:

> "Those who look to him are radiant; their faces are never covered with shame."
>
> Psalm 34:5.

Then I clicked on Heather Williams' video, *Hallelujah—Story Behind the Song.*

I found out Heather Williams had written this song a year after the passing of her baby boy. In her brokenness, she made a decision to feel the pain, to keep an open dialogue with God, to ask Jesus to show up right where she was, and yet still praise and love God for anything and everything. Heather had realized that through all of it, she could stand in God's Grace and by her willingness to speak and sing, she hoped that someone else could also stand in difficult circumstances. She recognized that when we are down, we need to let God reach in and we need to give our pain up to him. I was touched that it was a song about a parent child relationship and the profound loss of a loved one who had gone back home to God. God is great! Hallelujah!

To me, Hallelujah meant "Yayyy God!" or "Praise the Lord!" but I thought it might be useful to know more precisely. So I looked up the definition.

Hallelujah:

1. an expression of worship or rejoicing; praise, joy, or thanks;
2. praise ye, Yahweh (or Jehovah). Hallalu: to praise;
3. a musical composition expressing praise;
4. synonyms: glory (or glory be), ha (or hah), hooray, hey, hotdog, huzzah, wahoo, whee, whoopee, yahoo, yippee.

Well, that definition fit with my experience. I could even relate to "a musical composition expressing praise,"—definitely relevant since I was loving this song that was praising God. So, to me, "hallelujah" means to praise, to feel joy, and to give thanks to God. Glory be to God . . . Hallelujah!

On Monday October 4, when I started telling people about the song, I knew some people might think the experience was totally random or that it was just me perceiving (or rather misperceiving) that it was from God or what some people like to call "a God thing." Regardless, I was so excited by the whole experience that I sent an email out to my family and friends, which is not like me. I don't tend to put myself out there in such vulnerable ways. I have been told before that I tend to hide my light under a bushel. I would say that most people who know me, besides Michael and my two closest friends, don't really know the spiritual side of me that well. Only one family member replied to my email. I guess the rest just let it go, couldn't relate, or thought I was too out there—and perhaps cracking under the strain of my father's illness.

Sharing this story was definitely a step out of my comfort zone. I said to Michael, "It's like that saying: 'Why is it that when you talk to God, it's called praying but when God talks to you, you're nuts?'" What is the diagnosis when God plays music for you on the radio? The next night I was listening to Shine FM in the car and the DJ used the same quotation—only she used the term "schizophrenic" instead of "nuts." It seemed like reinforcement for my thoughts. Would people think I was crazy? At the time, on that Monday morning that felt like Easter Monday, I was so excited about all that had occurred I just didn't care . . . at all.

Later I realized that some people might think that it was just random or coincidence or they may question whether God really had anything to do with it. Two people said, they had heard that song frequently as well. Therefore, I was not the only one—the implication, of course, was that God was not playing that song for me. I know it could sound crazy to anyone who has not had a similar experience before. It does sound like someone in the beginning stages of developing a religious delusion. And because of my own rational, logical mind, there were times when I thought that as well. But once I saw the whole pattern leading up to that Friday night of my dad's spiritual healing and renewed physical strength, steroid or not, I could see God's hand in it. Hallelujah.

The reality was that most people didn't say anything. Silence can be deafening as well. I knew the truth.

In his book, *The Spontaneous Fulfillment of Desire*, Deepak Chopra discusses the spirituality of coincidence:

> When you live your life with an appreciation of coincidences and their meanings, you connect with the underlying field of infinite possibilities. This is when

the magic begins. This is a state I call synchrodestiny, in which it becomes possible to achieve the spontaneous fulfillment of our every desire. Synchrodestiny requires gaining access to a place deep within yourself, while at the same time awakening to the intricate dance of coincidences out in the physical world.

So, to me, coincidence can easily be, "a God thing."

I kept turning on the radio in the week that followed hoping to hear that song playing and never did. Ten days later, on Wednesday, October 13, I was leaving Grace's house after spending a few hours with her praying, strategizing, and talking about this song, my dad, and everything that had been happening. I got in my car and turned on the radio. It wasn't playing. Disappointed again, I said to God, out loud, "Okay God, I totally get it. It's not random or coincidence. It's totally you. It's for me and it's for Dad. Please play it again for me. There is no doubt in my mind!"

Four minutes later, it came on. HALLELUJAH!

And I knew: *Those who look to him are radiant; their faces are never covered with shame.* (Psalm 34:5).

In *Conversations with God*, Neale Donald Walsch writes: "Ask me anything. *Anything.* I will contrive to bring you the answer. The whole universe will I use to do this. So be on the lookout . . . You may ask a question . . . But Watch. Listen. The words to the next song you hear. The information in the next article you read. The story line of the next movie you watch. The chance utterance of the next person you meet. Or the whisper of the next river, the next ocean, the next breeze that caresses your ear—*all these devices* are Mine; all these avenues are open to Me. I will speak to you if you will listen. I will come to you if you will invite Me. I will show you then that I have *always* been there. *All ways.*"

On Friday October 1, I knew God was completely with us and I knew I could trust Him. It's not that I didn't before, but on that day, I could feel God's Grace even more strongly than before and I knew God was closer to my dad and as a result, to me as well. I had a real Easter Experience from Friday to Monday. Friday evening, it became apparent that it was God's Friday. I hope the Christians who read this are not offended. I'm not comparing my dad to Jesus Christ—it was just a powerful experience for me. Through Easter, God gave Christians, "a new birth into a living hope through the resurrection of Jesus Christ from the dead. Easter is about hope; hope that we may be spiritually resurrected with Jesus so we may walk in a new way of life." As we walk on our journey, adversity can fast track us in our growth with God and Jesus.

I reached a new level of being-ness with God through that time—and it was amazing. Hallelujah!

<u>Favorite Dad Memory:</u> I remember Dad carrying me on his shoulders up to the age of six or seven. It felt so wonderful to ride so high and hold on to my dad's forehead or under his chin. Sometimes his whiskers felt just a little rough. Dad always gave me that "being carried" feeling throughout my life. He was great with elevation. I always knew that Dad loved me, supported me, and wanted the best for me—it was unconditional.

Lesson: Unconditional love is a gift. God will carry you if you let Him.

Chapter 6

Onward

*The Lord is close to the broken-hearted and saves
those who are crushed in spirit.*

—Psalm 34:18

The Saturday after the amazing Friday night, Michael went to the hospital early to ensure Dad would not be moved to a different unit without our knowing. He also wanted to be there when the doctors arrived to (a) see the looks on their faces when they saw Dad, (b) discuss further tests, the pain medication and possible hallucinations, and (c) reinforce Dad's hope if he still had it and reignite it if he didn't.

After the Friday evening we experienced, we really had no idea what to expect. We could only hope and pray for improvement, while still knowing that decline was a distinct possibility. Sometimes, it's hard to be a realist.

My husband was great to me and my dad throughout this time. He supported me in in so many ways. Michael visited Dad with me and without me. He attended meetings with the doctors. He arranged things at the hospital. He was there to speak with me any time I needed and offered me his counsel and wisdom. He helped me look at things objectively. He helped out even more than usual at home and with whatever needed to be done. Michael hugged me and loved me and helped me to stay standing, especially when it looked like I might topple. He was just there for me, and there for my dad too. Hallelujah!

Before Michael left for the hospital, I sent out an email update about his mission and asked for prayer:

> *"Pray that Dad gets some strength to begin walking and moving more and pray that we find the right pain meds . . ."*

Dad had eaten well at breakfast. "I felt so much love from my family last night," he said.

"I agree with you," Michael replied.

"All of my family members are team players. I think I'm ready to be Wendy's project. Regaining energy and walking are my first priorities." An intern doctor came in and spent half an hour with them and Dad told him how he was feeling, about his care, and his opinions about the health care system.

"You are looking very well today, John," the intern said with some shock. He also seemed surprised with Dad's coherence.

"Thank you," Dad replied. "I want to work on getting out of bed and start walking again."

"I think that's a good idea," the doctor commented.

"I think that this crisis is pulling people together and connecting my whole family." Dad was back in the game.

Dad's family doctor stopped by to visit and encouraged Dad to think about what kind of things he wanted to do with his life. I liked that he didn't treat my father as a person without any purpose, who was just sick and dying—even if this could become or was the truth. I now know, though, that dying is purposeful too. Hallelujah.

That night, Dad was tired and his spirits weren't nearly as strong as they had been Friday night or that morning and afternoon. I had brought some of the strong liquid vitamin supplement with me to the hospital in a Tupperware container that I had bought a few weeks ago. I was hoping that he would be willing to try it. Dad didn't seem that enthusiastic about it and when I told him it was a very strong taste, he got sick to his stomach. Clearly, that was not going to work out. I had carried the supplement with me to and from the hospital many times with the hope that Dad would take it. One time it spilled inside my purse and stained the file folder containing my notes on cancer and Dad's case that I carried with me everywhere that I went. Still, when I look at that green file folder, which still contains the notes and papers from that time, I look at that stain. And when I look at that stain, I still see the quashed hope of the idea that I could actually help Dad heal from his dis-ease – a hope that I developed when he was diagnosed.

On Sunday, October 3, he looked better and stronger still, and Dad decided he would start trying to increase his strength. He did some leg exercises with Michael that morning, whom he appointed as his trainer. He was quite perky and very conversational while he was eating his lunch. The internist (Dr. Doom) stopped by to see Dad and looked quite surprised by his calmness, energy level, and cognitive capacity even though the doctor did not comment on this or ask to speak to any of us. Dad spoke for himself very effectively and asked about the possibility of a CT scan as well as having the nephrostomy tubes internalized. Dad was able to stand with the help of Michael and Robert—he even stood on his own on the weigh scale. Overall, I felt positive about his physical progression. I jokingly wrote in an email update:

> *"That Decadron/steroid is some fine stuff—I'd almost like to take some myself . . ."*

On Monday, October 4, Michael and I visited Dad in the morning. He looked really good and asked to get dressed. We were stunned! I realized the only clothes he had there were the sweatshirt and sweatpants he had been wearing when the ambulance brought him in on September 23. So Michael and I helped Dad get dressed and called Mom to request some clothes. Dad even specified what clothes he wanted. While this may seem trivial, it was major progress for us. Putting a sweatshirt on a man who could barely sit up by himself and who had an IV lead and two kidney bags was no easy task.

I filled in Dad's hospital meal order form and gave him some dietary advice, and he lovingly referred to me as his nutritionist. One of the interns stopped by to see Dad and was quite surprised. "Wow, you are looking good," he said. "I'm going to recommend that the kidney tubes be internalized since you have progressed so much. I recommend we get a physiotherapist to work with you. There might even be a chance that you could go home, with home care." That was a change in tune to be sure. I had to leave to pick up Arianna from school, but Michael stayed to work with Dad.

Michael called me later, excited to tell me how things had gone. He had been able to get my dad to stand up with his support. Great! Dad had taken five steps forward, assisted. Wow! And then five steps back. Incredible! Dad had taken ten steps forward. Get out! And then ten steps back. No way! Then Dad wanted to be taken out of his room in the wheelchair. Seriously?

Dad had wanted a tour of the ward, so they set off. Then Dad wanted to go to the chapel, much to Michael's surprise and marvel. When they arrived there, Dad asked the woman at the front, "I would like to speak to whoever was in charge here." The chaplain came out of his office.

"What can I do to help you Mr. Bennett?" the chaplain asked.

"I was wondering if it would it be okay if I could hold a choir practice for twenty guys tomorrow at one o'clock?" Dad inquired.

"No problem," the chaplain replied. "Perhaps we could open up the rehearsal to whoever would like to come and listen?"

"I hoped you would say that. That sounds great! Thank you," Dad said appreciatively.

Michael told me, "Your Dad had already made that plan for me to take him to the chapel. He knew exactly what he was doing— from getting dressed to booking the chapel. He was on a mission to make it happen." John Bennett was back in action.

I was ecstatic. It seemed nothing short of Amazing Grace. On Saturday, I had prayed and suggested we all pray that Dad would walk, and Monday, he was walking with support. I was walking on sunshine. In elation, I sent out an email update to family and friends:

> *I think the Decadron has given Dad a boost physically and cognitively. I could see Dad's physical progression from Friday, September 24 (nephrostomy tubes day), to last Thursday and Friday and saw him gaining physical strength but losing/not gaining any emotional or spiritual will to live. Friday was a definite turning point in his progression since he has found the will to live and the hope to try and the grace to accept whatever time and energy he has left to experience in his life, be that a very short term or longer term. I was overjoyed and I feel that God has answered our prayers, at least for now. My own experience of Friday night was an experience of a miracle. I felt God's presence in the room!*

In the same email, I described my experience with the song *Hallelujah*. Then I continued:

> *And so, it began the Friday night wonder . . . I just thought I would share that experience with you in case it was meaningful in any way. I normally am quite careful about what I tell most people about my experiences of God because some people don't have the ears to hear or the eyes to see and just assume you are crazy. In this case, I say, think whatever you like because I am crazy . . . crazy about JESUS!!!!!! There it is . . . AMEN.*

On Tuesday, Dad's choir rehearsal was held in the chapel. They were a small Barbershop chorus of mostly retired men. Dad started the group—a group which his close friends referred to as "The Old Farts." The rehearsal was wonderful to watch. Dad was in good spirits, and made jokes as he led his fellow barbershoppers in song. He not only sang and directed, but also made a speech about his journey from August 25th on, and how he felt he had experienced a miracle in his recovery. He credited and thanked me for saving his life on September 23. It was a lovely, profound moment. Dad made it through forty-five minutes of the one-hour rehearsal and then we took him back to his room. We got him out of the chair which had become very uncomfortable after so long. He looked tired but contented (and not as tired as I thought he would). That rehearsal had been a blessing. Hallelujah!

The palliative nurse called me that afternoon and requested a meeting with the family. I sent an email to my family to let them know. My mom was not keen on the idea of palliative care. I think for her, it meant end-of-life care which meant death, and that was just too hard for her to face. Who could blame her?

On Wednesday, Dad was tired from the rehearsal but he looked good and we had a nice conversation. "Wendy, I feel like my life is a symphony with the third movement missing," he told me.

"What do you mean?" I asked.

"I mean the kinds of things that make life interesting and fulfilling."

"Well, I think it is amazing that you can even think this way, given where you were last week. You've clearly already made a start with your idea to hold the rehearsal yesterday," I offered.

"I agree. I guess I'm just wondering where I will go from here."

When I went back later in the day, I asked Dad, "Do you want to go outside in the wheelchair for a breath of fresh air?"

"No, I don't think so, thanks. I'm a bit too tired. Maybe tomorrow?"

"Sure," I agreed. Why don't we fill out your menu plan for the week?"

As we were going through each meal, Dad paused and commented, "Oh I probably can't have this . . ." Then he stopped and looked up at me half expectantly. He looked like he might be asking me for something really difficult.

"Dad, I think you could ask me for just about anything and I would do whatever it took to get it for you!"

"Could I have some salt with my eggs?" he asked hopefully. *Salt*, I thought. *And he thought I would refuse him. Ha!* Of course, salt is an issue for a patient with severe kidney issues and edema.

"Sure Dad! You can have that if you want," I replied.

He beamed happily. Sometimes it is the little things that can add to our quality of life, and it is nice when we can be grateful for them.

On Thursday, we had the family meeting with the palliative team—a doctor, nurse, and student nurse. Before the meeting started, Dad told us he had been thinking about things he would like to do. In fact, he had written a list: play bridge, play chess, do other people's taxes/accounting, arrange music, and go bowling, to name a few. *Bowling*, I mused. *How did that make the list?* This was lovely to see him considering what he wanted and what might be possible.

Dad co-led the meeting with the palliative doctor and he requested better pain management. The doctor suggested switching from hydromorphone to fentanyl, as well as adding octreotide to help regulate bowel function. I sent an email update to my aunt and uncle (Dad's brother):

> *I thought the meeting went very well. Dad, Mom, Brian, Robert, Katherine, and I were all there in Dad's room with the palliative team/consults. The doctor really clarified the role of palliative care in Dad's case and tried to lay out a landscape for deciding where we go from here. The choices seem*

to be 1) stay in the hospital, 2) go to hospice, or 3) possibly go home. We discussed what we need to consider and how we should make that decision. Dad's goal is to get home if he can so I think that is what we are working towards. Dad fully participated in this meeting. Actually, I would have to say he even co-led the meeting with the doctor, and, in fact, adjourned the meeting.

Dad continues to progress physically and mentally from what I can see. I believe the next week will be telling. We will see if he continues to improve or stabilizes at a certain level. The doctor was also surprised to see Dad doing so well and did say, "It is a miracle." He said if he had given Dad a prognosis when Dad came in to the hospital he would have been wrong three times already. It also was co-incidental that this doctor had met Dad (sometime around 1980) while he was in med school. He wanted to do a barbershop number for a show he was involved in, and Dad was one of the barbershoppers that helped coach the group. Dad even remembered which song they sang.

The palliative doctor was not overly optimistic about Dad's prognosis and does not believe Dad will see an improvement in his various conditions, which he believes are all related to the spread of the cancer i.e., kidneys, bowel/rectum, abdomen/lymph nodes, liver, coccyx—all the places where Dad is in pain. The doctor thinks that we will not even see much improvement in Dad's blood protein levels or edema since he sees the cancer continually causing inflammatory cascade failure throughout Dad's body, especially in his internal organs. His approach is to see what they can do to maximize comfort and quality of life and minimize suffering. The palliative doctor's belief is that "when one of us suffers, we all suffer," which I appreciate. It is very spiritual in nature . . . nice to see/experience with a westernized medical doctor.

The doctor has put Dad on a hormone called octreotide, which he hopes will regulate the bowel. I am really hoping this is the case since the whole bowel/diarrhea issue has been such a quality of life issue for Dad and his care. If this could be *resolved in any fashion it would be a big step forward for Dad. The doctor also suggested regular, as needed, blood transfusions since Dad is anemic (it seems like they have also taken enough blood from Dad to transfuse somebody else) and he is hoping this will also add to Dad's improvement. He told us that Dad's kidneys are functioning at 30% which is a big improvement over the less than 5% two weeks ago, but they are still not as strong as we would hope. The doctor also wants to take Dad off of the dilaudid (morphine derivative) pain killer and put him on fentanyl—since Dad is still experiencing pain—with the aim to find a dose that maximizes pain management and cognitive functioning.*

We also discussed having a cancer specialist brought in, which may happen. The doctor was not all that hopeful that a cancer doc would be able to add/change anything, but he did show some willingness to do so if this is what we want, so this is a possibility.

I also inquired about the hospital's stance on complementary/naturopathic options and it seems like there may be some possibilities there. I still have some belief that some small measures may be able to bring small improvements and I will discuss those with Dad/docs perhaps today. At this point, I would be willing to try many things if I were in Dad's place. I still have the belief that inflammatory cascade failure can change to inflammatory cascade improvement although I am grounded in the reality of where we are at/Dad is at, at this point in his disease progression.

So, we are at an interesting point, hopeful with the amazing progress/turnaround/miracle/healing of Dad's spirit and heart we experienced starting last Friday and yet still grounded in the reality of the cancer dis-ease.

And so we move onward . . .
Love for now . . . Wendy :)

In the meeting, Mom had said to Dad, "You've got another miracle coming," which even caught me by surprise. No one in the room disagreed. I didn't know about the others, but I was still seeing this as a possibility. It was hopeful. I asked the palliative doctor at the end of the meeting if the Decadron was responsible for Dad's improvement. He said it could be part of it but that Dad's reaction to it was not typical. This led me to think the improvement had more to do with God than the steroid—or it was at least a combination of the two.

Every step of the way, managing the drugs and pain medications was a challenge. We all tried to stay on top of what Dad was being given and why, but it was difficult—some of the staff were very cooperative and competent, others not so much. The issues of bowel function and pain management always seemed to be our Mount Everest that we never seemed to be able to climb.

On Friday, October 8, we all noticed that Dad's spirits were considerably lower, and we were unsure whether it was the change in pain medication, the ongoing rectal pain, the diarrhea issue, or everything combined. The diarrhea was really, really disheartening for my father, and we all wished that more could be done to help him. I was somewhat focused on trying to implement some complementary therapies that I had read about weeks earlier. I asked Robert to bring green tea, probiotics, evening primrose oil, and melatonin. It wasn't much, but it was a start.

The next day, Michael went to the hospital with a chess board, intent on having a game with Dad as chess was on Dad's list of things he wanted to do. Michael said Dad was in great spirits—almost the best he had seen yet. This was very encouraging, even though they never did play a game of chess.

Brian visited later that day and said Dad was in a bad way spiritually. How quickly things can change. Dad's pain was very bad, and he felt he had limited hope for improvement. He said several times he wanted to die, and again he asked to see the chaplain.

Dad had developed a thrush infection on his rear end, and his pain level went through the roof. He rated it a ten out of ten and said it felt as if his skin was on fire. We all knew a ten on the

John Bennett Scale of Pain must have been horrendous! When the internist stopped by to see him, Dad wept in desperation. The internist increased his medication by 67 percent, which seemed to help, and he added codeine to the mix to try to tighten up the GI tract. We wondered, again, if the bowel issues were due to the cancer, to certain medications, or to another underlying condition such as an infection, perforation, or secondary disease.

On Sunday, Michael made it clear to the head nurse that we wanted to see a GI as soon as possible and that we wanted family members present for the consult. Dad's pain level was a four or a five that morning. He acknowledged that the family's positive support and encouragement had been helpful the previous day, even though the day had become progressively worse and discouraging for him. Dad told Michael that some of the nurses had told him he had the best family they had ever seen. They said that they had some patients who never got any visitors at all (one man had been there three months without a single visitor—very sad).

Brian visited in the afternoon and said Dad felt worse again. He seemed to be in more pain and had little hope for improvement. He wept several times, again said that he wanted to die, and that he wanted to see the chaplain. The diarrhea was still problematic and now the bed-sores he had developed on his lower back were worse.

Brian said that Dad looked better in the evening and that the thrush infection had improved somewhat. Dad seemed more comfortable and in better spirits, but he still wanted spiritual counseling to help him cope with his conflicted feelings of wanting to live and yet wanting to die. The nurse put a note on his chart requesting a spiritual consult first thing in the morning. Brian said that observing this improvement reinforced for him that if we could manage Dad's pain, then his misery would be easier to manage as well, and Dad would be better able to fight the good fight.

We still wanted additional tests and exams with regard to the bowel issue and the cancer, although we realized at the time, and even moreso after the fact, that the doctors were not really interested in further assessment. Michael's request for a GI consult was rejected—they thought it was unnecessary and that nothing could be done. It is difficult to know if they were right or not. I wondered if the staff might also consider us annoying, in addition to supportive.

It seemed they had more or less written Dad off, so to speak. At one point we wanted a second CT scan done to see if there was any improvement, but the doctors did not agree. They didn't say so, but I believe they would have considered it a poor use of valuable medical resources. There were times when I even wondered if they just wanted their hospital bed back. But perhaps that is pragmatic in a system of limited resources.

I continually struggled to figure out if Dad could make any progress through either medical treatment or God's healing power. All the information in front of me suggested he was in end-stage cancer and very close to dying. It was a hard line to walk.

From October 1 to October 11, 2010, Dad was with us. He was struggling but he was with us, and I believe he was ready or trying to be ready for whatever Our Lord was planning for him. I felt like we were all waiting to see if there would be any further miraculous improvements on a path toward healing, or if he would continue to be ill and prepare to finish his life on earth and go home to God.

During this time, I realized that I had to live as if my dad would be healed so that I didn't fall into mourning before his time came. I wanted to hang on to hope even though I wasn't able to do so much of the time. I tried to discern what God was leading us to, but I really was not sure and had to prepare for whatever result was to come. I was still praying for healing and a really big miracle.

<u>Favorite Dad Memory:</u> My dad had social grace and appreciated it in others. He would shake your hand or give you a hug when he saw you. Even when the doctors came into his hospital room, whenever he was strong enough, he extended his arm to shake their hands. Dad typically sent me a thank-you note/email after coming to my house for dinner, and whenever he spoke to me, I felt important. I sometimes teased him, saying there is no such thing as a "civil" engineer (his first degree at McGill University), but in fact, he was very civilized—civilized meaning he was cultured and intellectually advanced. Dad always signed his emails to us "Harmoniously, With Love, Dad."

Lesson: God's Grace can shine through each of us in small and big ways.

Chapter 7

Thanksgiving

. . . but we also rejoice in our sufferings, because we know that suffering produces endurance; and endurance produces character; and character produces hope. And hope does not disappoint us, because God has poured out his love into our hearts through the Holy Spirit, whom he has given us.

—Romans 5:3-5 (RSV)

October 11, was Thanksgiving Monday. A few days earlier, Michael and I had thought that it would be nice to have a Thanksgiving gathering in Dad's hospital room since he couldn't be with us for our traditional Thanksgiving dinner at home. I knew Dad had been looking for the hospital chaplain on several occasions and so I thought, *if he can't go to church and the chaplain's not available, then maybe I can bring a little church to him.* I planned for prayer and communion followed by my version of worship singing. I had never led a prayer with my family or performed a communion ritual. I had never played guitar and sang in front of them either.

Due to Dad's up-and-down condition on Saturday and Sunday, we weren't sure if we would be able to go ahead with our plans, so Michael went to the hospital Monday morning to see how he was feeling. Michael texted me to give me the go-ahead as Dad was in pretty good spirits. Grace had given me communion oil and water that she had brought back from Israel, but she had borrowed them from me, so I went over to her house that Monday morning to pick them up. She gave me a lovely little communion kit—the label read, "A Blessing from the Holy Land." Perfect. There were three items in the kit: Water from the holy Jordan River, Wine from Cana of Galilee, and Oil from the Church of the Holy Sepulchre. We prayed together and she asked God, "to give us the day and make it His." What a beautiful friend. Grace had walked the cancer journey with me the whole way. Her support, prayers, and love were unfailing.

Michael and I had also planned for Michael, Brian, and Katherine to play a game of bridge with Dad before we all gathered in Dad's room. However, there was a miscommunication between me and Brian—he didn't receive my email in time. But perhaps it was providence. Dad probably would have struggled to play bridge with the extensive medication he was taking.

We all started arriving after eleven o'clock and we talked and laughed with Dad. Once everyone was there, we began our service.

We joined hands in a circle around Dad's bed and I prayed:

> *Dear Father, Dear Holy Spirit, Dear Jesus, we ask for your presence among us, O God, Creator of the Universe, Sustainer of Life, Redeemer of Humankind. Please bring your healing light and power into our wounded hearts and bodies and minds and souls and clear the way for each of us to discover the fullness of your power and all of your wondrous blessings. Help us dear God to receive and share your love so that we may be a beacon through which you may shine into the world so that we may be the hands and feet of Christ and be part of your Kingdom both in Heaven and on Earth. Let us give thanks to the Lord, our God, Emmanuel—God is with us.*

Then we paused for a minute or two and prayed in silence.

We each silently bring our prayers to you ... Amen.

I continued:

Jesus took the bread, gave thanks to You, broke the bread, gave it to his disciples and said: Take, eat, this is my body which is given to you. Do this in remembrance of me. Then he took the cup, gave thanks to You, gave it to his disciples and said: Do this in remembrance of me.

In remembrance of these, your mighty acts in Jesus Christ, we offer ourselves in praise and Thanks-giving in union with Christ's offering for us as we proclaim the mystery of faith. Pour out your Holy Spirit on us gathered here and on these gifts of bread and wine. By your Spirit, make us one with Christ, one with each other, and one in ministry to all the world. The bread which we break; it is a means of sharing in the body of Christ. The cup over which we give thanks; it is a means of sharing in the outpoured blood of Christ.

Michael passed out the bread, and our son David held the cup of wine for each of us to dip the bread. With the oil, I marked each of us with a cross on the forehead and said, "You are anointed in Him." Then I continued:

The title Christ is derived from the Hebrew, "Messiah" and means literally "covered in oil; anointed." The anointing which you have received from Him abides in you. 1 John 2:27 (NRSV). I anoint you with this oil in the name of the Father, the Son, and the Holy Spirit. May you receive the fullness of His blessings and joy.

We ask for your presence among us, O Lord; God of Wonder and God of Light. We ask you to be with us and share this time with us. As we journey together, it is your

Grace that sustains us and carries us forward. Thank you for
all the blessings you give us.

Then we sang and I played guitar. Of the four of us kids, I am
the least musically trained. Growing up, I spent more time in
tap dance classes than I did in guitar lessons. However, from my
limited repertoire I chose three songs: "Let It Be," "The Rainbow
Connection," and "Day By Day."

There is great wisdom in the song "Let It Be": "When I find
myself in times of trouble . . . in my hour of darkness . . . when
the night is cloudy there's still a light that shines on me," and the
wisdom of the Universe says, let it be.

During this time, we really were living "Day by Day," and
the words from this song from *Godspell*, reminded me to pray for
three things: "to see Thee more clearly, love Thee more dearly,
follow Thee more nearly." I am still praying for these things day
by day.

"What's on the other side," of the "Rainbow Connection," and
how do we find it? Kermit the Frog sang this song in *The Muppet
Movie*. It was an excellent choice because Dad used to teach that
song to the kids in his ukulele class. "What's so amazing that keeps
us star gazing and what do we think we might see? I've heard
them (voices) calling my name . . . too many times to ignore it.
It's something that I'm supposed to be." What a sweet song about
the mysteries of life, searching for truth, listening for the call,
and following your heart, knowing that sometimes we have more
questions than answers.

Even though these were not standard church hymns, I felt
a great deal of Spirit and Grace as we sang together. Later, I
concluded that the message of the music was this: let it be, as we
see, love, and follow God day by day, and wonder what's on the
other side.

After prayer, communion, and music, we ate the small picnic
that we had brought with us. Afterwards, Brian picked up the guitar

and started playing. Katherine, Brian, and I sang a barbershop song called "A Little Bit" that we all used to sing together as a family. The singer talks about his father, a preacher, who spreads the word through this song—and "when daddy dies," he promises to still sing it so his voice will still be heard.

A little bit of happiness, a little less sadness
A little bit of all these things don't happen overnight
A little bit of tenderness, a little less bitterness
A little bit of all these things going to make this world alright.

I had thought about singing this song a few days before but I remembered the second verse said, "when Daddy died I promised him that his voice would still be heard." I thought it might not be a great idea to sing about "Daddy dying." We sang it anyway.

This gathering was a joyful few moments in time that we were able to spend together with God in Thanks-giving despite the bleak and difficult times we found ourselves in. Hallelujah.

Despite the fact that Dad had requested a chaplain visit a few times, and his personal directive requested pastoral care, we never managed to make this happen. So I was very happy that we were able to spend time together as a family and give Dad spiritual care. The nurse had made a note of his request for a spiritual consult the night before Thanksgiving—maybe what we provided was the consult Dad was supposed to have.

<u>Favorite Dad Memory:</u> One time, while visiting my dad in the hospital, a male nurse walked in to check on him. Exchanging pleasantries, he teased Dad, "How did an old codger like you get such a beautiful daughter?" Dad replied, "I married well." We laughed and then he added, "She's beautiful on the inside too." He gave me an endearing look and smile. That was who my dad was.

Lesson: Who you really are on the inside is far more important than how you look on the outside.

Chapter 8

Post Thanksgiving

Don't panic. I'm with you. There's no need to fear for I'm your God.
I'll give you strength. I'll help you. I'll hold you steady
and keep a firm grip on you.

—Isaiah 41:10 (MSG)

On the morning of Tuesday, October 12, Dad was fairly sedated—perhaps overmedicated, which was far better than undermedicated. I wondered whether the medication was administered by the doctors or requested by Dad. Katherine and Mom were planning to be at the hospital throughout the day in hopes of connecting with the doctors, who tended to be somewhat elusive. If you didn't catch them on their rounds, you would be left sitting around wondering what was going on. Some of the nurses were very good and some inspired less confidence. Useful information was hard to come by and keep track of. The diarrhea issue had shown some improvement—measures taken seemed to be working.

I had brought pomegranate juice and a greens supplement with me to the hospital for Dad. I had talked to him a few days earlier and had gone over some complementary therapies that we could try. I had many ideas but I knew time was not on my side. I sent an email out to my family asking if they were on board, but I didn't get much response. It was hard to know what everybody else was thinking. From my point of view, we had nothing to lose and our dad to gain. I still felt there was a chance . . . however minuscule or minute.

On Wednesday, one of the resident doctors stopped by. He was still focused on getting the bowel working properly, and he added Imodium to the mix. The palliative specialist decreased the dosage of pain meds slightly and suggested a topical morphine cream for the thrush infection on Dad's posterior. This seemed like a very good idea. Another doctor stopped by and was only concerned about Dad's comfort, which my mom did not like. She was not ready to give up hope.

On Thursday, I realized he was sleeping a great deal and did not have the same energy he had been gaining the week before. Dad seemed to have spiraled down slightly and then stabilized in groggy. The previous week's improvement seemed to have evaporated. The diarrhea was still an issue, sadly. The codeine had been stopped, and the palliative doctor had added Haldol to his treatment, which for some reason I didn't feel comfortable with. I made a mental note to myself to Google Haldol when I got home.

The nurse came in to clean him up.

"I don't want to be cleaned," Dad said emphatically. "In fact, I'm not going to be," he stated assertively. I knew it was very painful on his backside. *Who could blame him*, I thought. My heart ached for him.

"I promise I'll be really gentle," the nurse countered.

"No," Dad stated. I had to admire his tenacity.

"Remember the pain and the burning, on fire feeling on Saturday night due to the infection? It will be much better if you get it over with quickly rather than wait and let it all get worse again," I persuaded. He stopped arguing and relented. I waited outside.

"I want to review my situation with you," Dad said after.

"Okay," I replied.

"I'm feeling hopeless. Maybe someone from palliative care might be able to help. I don't think the hospital can offer me anything further."

Matthew, the neighbor who had prayed with us on the lawn beside the ambulance, on September 23, appeared at the door. "Is it okay if I stop in to visit?" he asked. He reminded Dad of the trials of Job and David, and he read a verse in the Bible reminding us that there is no sickness in Heaven. A timely visit.

After he left, I asked Dad, "Do you feel there is any point to your suffering?"

"I'm not sure," he replied.

"Do you think there are any lessons in what you are experiencing and all you've had to go through?" I queried.

"I think I've learned much more about humility. I definitely can relate to Job." Dad continued, "What do you think I should do?"

"Well, I think we should keep working on getting the right medications, especially for pain. And we should keep trying to resolve the diarrhea issue and improve bowel function. It might be a good idea to see the palliative doctor. There's a different doctor starting on the next rotation soon. What do you think you should do?"

"I would like to go to a hospice since I probably can't go home. It would be too much for Diana and Robert, even though I would like to go home," he said somewhat regretfully.

"Well, you were much closer to going home with your progress last week, compared to now."

"I agree," he said solemnly.

I was at the hospital every day, sometimes twice a day and Dad was either sleeping, or awake and coherent—I wouldn't have characterized him as delirious. On Friday, October 15, I had asked the palliative doctor if we could go back to the previous medications and reduced dosages, but he wouldn't budge. His response included something about "families feeling desperate," and after the discussion, I felt he had dismissed my opinions as acts of desperation. I felt I had been *managed* by the doctor—isn't that what doctors need to do with family members who create problems or question their judgment? I asked the doctor about the possibility of moving Dad to a hospice, and he essentially said it was too late and that moving him would not be a good idea.

I told Michael about the addition of the Haldol and he was shocked. He told me he didn't think it was a good choice since it was typically used for antipsychotic behavior. Of course—I knew I had heard of it before—when I was studying psychology in Grad school. Antipsychotic medications, such as Haldol, can knock you out, trigger psychosis (if you are not psychotic), or more rarely, stabilize your condition—what the doctor was hoping for.

I discussed the issue with Mom and Katherine, and we decided to request it be stopped until we could speak again with the palliative doctor the next day. Our goal had been to bring Dad's pain meds back down to a lower level. Michael and I believed that he was overmedicated and groggy but I thought the doctors believed that the sudden downturn was due to the cancer.

On Saturday, not only did the palliative doctor not want to stop the Haldol, he wanted to increase the dosage, in a move towards full sedation. Finally, we were able to reduce the fentanyl and officially stop the Haldol, but it was not easy to get the doctors to agree.

When we reviewed the medication levels with the doctor, I did the math and realized that Dad's meds had increased six-fold on the Thanksgiving weekend. When Dad asked for additional pain meds at the palliative meeting, the doctor put him on fentanyl with the hydromorphone as an "as needed" back-up. Fentanyl is three times the strength of hydromorphone. That same day, the internist nearly doubled the fentanyl and doubled the hydromorphone dose for the pain of the thrush infection. Then the codeine was added. By Tuesday, Dad was sleeping most of the time, not surprisingly.

Then after administering the Haldol on Thursday, they concluded that Dad was delirious and needed more Haldol. I realized the downturn in his condition could have been due to the cancer but if it was due to the six-fold increase in pain medication plus Haldol, then we could have been pulling Dad out of a morphine stupor. In any case, we thought reducing the meds was worth trying for twenty-four to forty-eight hours to see how he progressed while keeping an active watch on his pain levels. On the back burner was a plan for full sedation if Dad needed it. We felt somewhat comforted knowing we could manage his suffering.

Finally, the diarrhea seemed to be under control and the thrush infection had improved. Dad slept through the morning visit while we were there, but I had a very nice visit with him that evening— the nicest visit since Thanksgiving Monday.

On Sunday, I sent out an email update:

> It is a tricky process with many docs, nurses, specialists etc involved. In an Alberta hospital you are mostly at the mercy of the doctors and trying to be there when they show up. You walk the line between being a concerned family and an annoying, intrusive, difficult, deluded, desperate family . . . I'm fairly certain we have all of those labels.
>
> Despite the push in the Alberta Health Region for patient-centered and family-centered care, it has definitely not been achieved, but we will keep striving to that end.
>
> It is clear to me that the docs have no hope for him . . . everything they do is clearly palliative . . . the doctors have no hope for any kind of a cure but are expecting total decline, and I don't believe they will see Dad as anything but terminal (even with his upswing Oct 1). In fact, I get the feeling sometimes that they would just like their hospital bed back . . .
>
> The only hope for Dad's recovery in my estimation would be a miracle cure, and after witnessing what happened to Dad on Friday, Oct 1, I have not ruled that out completely (surprising given my academic background but not at all given my spiritual background). Three weeks ago I had to learn to walk in the duality of knowing Dad could die any day while hoping that he would turn around and improve . . . the reality

of what is with the hope of what could be (and not premature grief). There are documented cases of people surviving advanced cancer, particularly stage IV prostate cancers. In fact, there is no cancer or stage of cancer that has not been survived (defined by 5 yrs. of life). I'm sure at Dad's advanced stage of disease, there are not many stories of survival . . . the doctors are grounded in the reality of what they have seen and experienced, I am sure.

Generally, we are trying to improve his quality of life in any way that we can and hope for the best optimal functioning in as pain-free and suffering-free a manner as possible. If we resolve the diarrhea/bowel issue to any degree that would be a huge step forward in quality of life for Dad . . . we have made inroads.

On Monday, Mom, Katherine and I met with a different palliative doctor due to the shift rotation. She didn't seem to like the fact that we had questions as well as our own ideas of what we wanted to see. In fact, many of the doctors did not appreciate it when I did not take their opinions over my own. I don't usually mind when people underestimate me. Sometimes it can even be an advantage—but this wasn't one of those times.

Over the past few weeks it had become very clear that we, as a family, had become experts on my dad's day to day condition and could provide information regarding his care that the doctors and nurses might not have. The nurses and doctors changed with the shifts and rotations, and the doctors, typically, only saw Dad for five minutes per day. The need for patient advocacy became very clear, which I had heard from other people before.

The palliative doctor made a reference to Dad's kidneys being in greater distress and I inquired about his creatinine levels. She looked on the chart and said it was 209 (the best it had been was 175). The graph she showed me exhibited a fairly flat line since the creatinine came down from 1500 on September 23. I wasn't seeing the increasing kidney failure but perhaps she wasn't explaining the issue well enough.

Katherine wanted to change Dad's care designation from M1 back up to R3—medical to some resuscitation. Mom agreed—we were tired of the doctors just humoring us and being unwilling to expend any resources on a patient they had concluded could die any time. With Dad's personal directive, we had all agreed that M1 was appropriate. However, I agreed with Katherine and began to think we shouldn't have accepted that change as easily as we did a few weeks earlier. We felt as though we had agreed to certain things inadvertently, and in the same situation again, I would keep the care level higher. The doctor did not agree with us but she did as we wished. Also, the morphine cream that had been discussed, but never delivered, was apparently on the way finally.

Tuesday October 19, I had spoken with the palliative doctor on the phone and she did not sound happy—her frustration was evident. Perhaps she was tired of our questions and opposition. Or perhaps her conversation with my mom had been difficult—Mom was not happy with the doctors so Mom might have been too direct. Having the palliative doctor unhappy with you is a bit like having the tooth fairy or the Easter Bunny mad at you because you were too confrontational. She mentioned again her many years of experience and the hours she had spent with our family. I wanted to correct her and say, "You mean hour," but thought it best to let it go and just accept that perhaps the less than one hour she had spent with Mom, Katherine, and I yesterday and the two phone calls that day, felt like hours and hours with the family. At least she didn't use the term, "You people . . ."

What was interesting is that both the doctor and Dad's day nurse said that Dad was improving slightly if you just looked at his chart and considered blood work and other measures. While I was visiting on Tuesday, Dad took his gown off in preparation for making a break for the door.

"You hold her and I'll go," Dad said. I assumed he was referring to the nurse standing on the other side of the bed. I'm not sure if he was joking or not. His abdomen actually looked better and much less inflamed compared to the week before, and he was able to sit up, something I hadn't seen in eight days.

If I hadn't seen the upswing on October 1, I would definitely have been lacking hope and motivation to seek improvement. But because I had, I was still thinking it was worth tweaking things to see if we could regain the ground we had lost since last Tuesday. Perhaps we could not . . . but what if we could?

What if God's plan was to heal Dad? I knew at that point that it would take a miracle. A Big Miracle! I figured if God's plan was to take Dad home to Heaven, then this would become evident. Like my mom, I still was not ready to give up hope. I had read on one cancer website that as long as someone is breathing, it is never too late to try to intervene, no matter how much of a long shot. Dad was still breathing but I did have to concede, it did not look good . . . at all.

<u>Favorite Dad Memory:</u> When I was thirteen or fourteen, I had a conversation with Dad about what career I might choose. I was concerned because I was in grade nine and didn't know which direction I was headed in. He told me not to worry—he said I had lots of time to figure it out. "You can do anything in the world that you want to—as long as you are willing to work for it," Dad encouraged me. He taught me that I could choose whatever career I wanted, as long as I did the best that I could in whatever I undertook.

Lesson: Figure out what you want and go after it with your whole heart.

Chapter 9

The Beginning of the End

The Lord is my strength and shield.
I trust Him with all my heart.

—Psalm 28: 7 (NCV)

The next day, Wednesday, October 20, Dad had had enough.

"It's time for me to go," he told Katherine.

"Hospice Dad?" Katherine replied.

"No."

"Your house?"

"No."

"You mean Heaven Dad?"

"Yes," Dad answered.

Katherine told us that this conversation was 100 percent clear and 100 percent Dad—she knew that he really meant it. Katherine thought that maybe he could be given a sedative until we could all decide together if there was anything else we could do. As it turned out, there really wasn't anything. Dad had hung on as long as he could, but the fight was over and the transition had begun.

While I was there in the afternoon, Dad woke up and said, "Help me, help me." There didn't seem to be anything anyone could do, so I put on the Masters' Singers CD and held his hand while he slept. Brian visited that night and wrote down that Dad was a bit fidgety, moaned a little, and was breathing irregularly. I think the nurse observed that Dad may be in the Cheyne-Stokes breathing pattern: quick, shallow, irregular breaths typical of someone who is dying. This breathing can occur hours or days before someone passes. Brian left shortly before one a.m. and wrote on Dad's chart, "Not tonight I think—heading home."

On Thursday, the nurse told me that Dad had been restless the previous night so they had increased his meds and added midazolam, the alternative to Haldol. Despite the fact that we were fairly certain Dad would pass within the next few days, Michael and I struggled with the fact that Dad was heavily sedated and did not have a feeding tube. That evening, Michael and I felt very uneasy about the fact that we could be starving him to death. But we knew that being intubated would be invasive and likely counterproductive at that point. More uncertainty. I discussed it with other family members and they seemed to be against the idea of a feeding tube, but I was still conflicted.

Thursday night, Brian wrote in Dad's chart again, "Going home—not tonight." My brother knew that the passing would not happen on the Wednesday or Thursday but the notes he left were ironic. Brian referred to himself going home, and it also seemed to be a secondary reference to Dad going home—to Heaven. Not tonight. The breathing pattern continued. The indicators were there that Dad did not seem to have long.

On Friday morning, I woke up and prayed. I asked God what to do. I felt like I needed to check in with three people: Michael, Grace, and Angela (my near-death experience friend from October 1). Michael was in a meeting, so I left him a message.

I called Grace and we talked for a long time—she did not feel hopeful. We decided to pray together. Then while I was on hold for a moment, I lit three candles and gathered my Bible, rosary beads from Jerusalem that Grace had given me, the mandala that Elena had given, and two crosses. I turned off the TV and turned the clock radio on—I wasn't sure why. While I was building my altar for God, a song came on the radio called "Out of My Hands" which I later learned is by the band Jars of Clay. Some of the lyrics caught my attention: "I wasted a rescue. Abandoned the mission. I've failed by my own hand and watched it all go wrong . . . And it's out of my hands. It was from the start." Perhaps it was out of my hands and it had been from the start.

Grace prayed with me and we both felt a sense of peace around my dad's passing. Then she did a truth-seeking exercise with me. First she made a case for letting him go and then a case for holding on. My gut reaction was slightly stronger for letting go. We both felt that we could wait twenty-four hours and then reassess the feelings with regard to the feeding tube.

I spoke to Michael after that and he still felt the same way: starving Dad to death without full sedation seemed inhumane, and like a horrible substitute for euthanasia. I later spoke to Angela and she told me to trust myself. She reinforced my feeling that I could wait one more day. Michael agreed.

On the way to the hospital on Friday night, I heard the same Jars of Clay song again. And again I was reminded "it's out of my hands, it was from the start." I was okay—I knew I could let Dad pass. I did not need to hold on. I was in touch with the reality of his diseased state and I knew it would take a spectacular miracle for him to survive and be well. The story of Lazarus came to mind— Jesus brought Lazarus back from the dead. I wasn't counting on that, but I still felt that anything was possible with God.

Grace's mother had gone home to God on August 7, 2008, with Grace by her side. On that day in 2008, Grace discussed her experiences with me, as well as with her sister and three other friends who had been at the hospital with her. She shared with me all the things she had said to her sweet mama.

"Grace, you were your mom's death coach," I told her. "We have birth coaches and life coaches—why not death coaches as well!" I said, as the six of us sat at the table discussing her Mom's passing.

"Yes, exactly! That's the subject of my doctoral dissertation. Death Coaching," one of Grace's friends chimed in. Amazing Grace. I had my best friend's experience to draw on.

While visiting Dad on that Thursday and Friday, I spent some time alone with him, and played the Master's Singers CD, as well as "Above All" by Michael W. Smith to soothe both of us. I hoped they were as comforting to him as they were to me.

On Friday, I had my communion oil from the Church of Sepulchre and water from the Jordan River. With the oil, I marked Dad's forehead with a cross and said, "You are anointed in Him." I sprinkled water on his head and feet and reminded him, "You are baptized in the Holy Spirit."

As strange as it may sound, on Thursday I decided to write the words "Grace," "Harmony," and "Love" on Dad's abdomen with a marker. I realize this may sound odd but I didn't think anyone would notice with the possible exception of the nurses. I had been thinking about it for many weeks—it was one of many interventions I had wanted to try. The idea came from the DVD, *What the Bleep Do We Know*, a docudrama that explores the idea of how our thoughts affect our bodies. I had given Dad the book version for Christmas one year. When I first found out that Dad had cancer, I had thought of writing positive words on his body particularly where the cancer was concentrated, inspired by a scene in the movie. Grace, Harmony, and Love—my wish for him in his body and on his journey. As I stared at the writing I realized the words embodied who my dad was for me. It was a profound moment.

I wrote some scripture on the whiteboard on the wall of Dad's room:

Trust in the Lord with all your heart and lean not unto your own understanding. In all your ways, acknowledge Him, and He shall direct your paths.

—*Proverbs 3:5 (HNV)*

Be still and know that I am God.

—*Psalm 46:10*

I am the way, the truth, and the life.

—*John 14:6*

I wanted to say good-bye and I wanted to give Dad permission to go. While Dad slept, I spent some time whispering to him things I wanted to tell him:

I love you, Dad, and I know you have always loved me. Thank you for being such a great dad.

You used all your gifts while you were here—your personality which made you endearing and authoritative at the same time, your keen intellect, your creative/artistic/musical talent, your ability to love gently and quietly . . . . your soulfulness.

This body has served you well. It is okay if it is finished and has had enough. Even in its brokenness and state of disease it has served you with gifts you have received in the last month—a renewed closeness in your relationships with family and friends, healing in your marriage, lessons in humility, and heightened Grace connecting you more fully with Jesus and God, preparing you for the transition to come.

It is okay if you have to leave us now. God loves you and Jesus loves you. I know God misses us when we are here and not with Him in Heaven—He will welcome you home. Soon God will have you and we will be the ones missing you . . . Until we meet again.

<u>Favorite Dad Memory:</u> When I was sixteen, I must have been looking quite serious and thoughtful at times because Dad said to me, "A little introspection is good, but be careful not to become too introspective—you can get lost in it." This was true for me then, perhaps it is still.

Around the same time, I had been wrestling with the meaning of life. One day, we were all playing bridge at home, and I started talking about how meaningless life could be—how we are born, go to school for thirteen to twenty years, work in jobs we don't like until we retire at an old age and our bodies start deteriorating until we die. No one else at the table seemed to pay too much attention to what I was saying, even though I was on a bit of a tirade. Then I asked, "What's it all for, anyways?" Dad replied calmly and coolly, "It's the only game in town."

Lesson: It is what it is. Simple yet profound.

Chapter 10

The End and the Beginning

Peace is not the absence of affliction
but the presence of God.

—Unknown

Both Katherine and Brian knew that Friday night was the night—the Holy Spirit was speaking to both of them, I think. Katherine had wanted to leave for home, but felt she couldn't go. Then Brian arrived and she left him with Dad after eleven o'clock.

At around 3:20 a.m. on Saturday October 23, I woke up (perhaps nudged by God or Dad). I walked into the bathroom. A few minutes passed and then I heard the phone ring. A phone ringing in the middle of the night was bound to mean one thing. It was Brian. Dad had gone home to be with God. Brian later told us that after Dad had passed, he felt a hand on his shoulder, but no physical body was there. Was it God? Was it Dad? Hallelujah!

I believe that being with someone when they pass over to the other side is a sacred privilege, as it is to be present when someone is born. Each death experience is unique, just like each birth experience. I believe, though, that it is hard for the person who is passing to leave when someone who loves him is there if that someone desperately wants him to live and not die. For all those people who feel awful because they weren't there when a loved one passed—I don't think you should feel guilty. I hadn't wanted Dad to die alone but now I realize it would have been fine either way. God was with him. Hallelujah!

Thanksgiving Day was the last day I spent with Dad when he was so enlivened by God's Grace. He mostly slept from then on and never had quite the same alertness when awake, though we did still have a few nice conversations. We had eleven days of Grace and I cherish that! Hallelujah.

I wish the story had ended with:

> . . . *and right when he was on the brink of death, God healed my dad. Dad is alive and healthy today, cancer-free!*

This would have been a fantastic ending to my story. It would have been an especially fantastic ending for my mom and our family, but what I like to remember is that the reality was a fantastic ending for my dad. He is now with Our Father in Heaven. Hallelujah.

Perhaps, to some who read this story, it won't seem like there was anything miraculous involved. After all, my dad died. God did not heal his physical body. However, I feel that God's presence with me throughout the ten-week ordeal was a divine gift in my life. I can't speak for the rest of my family, or for Dad, but I felt God's Love and Grace around me so much of the time, in a way I never had before. I felt like I was walking in a bubble of God's Grace that whole time. And I still feel surrounded by His Grace. There were times when I thought I could feel people praying for me. That was powerful! I had never felt that before.

I experienced "Footprints in the Sand"—God carried me through the most difficult time of my life. I didn't have to reach for His hand or ask Him to carry me or help me. God was there. God reached for my hand before I reached or looked for His. God acted like we hope our spouses and best friends will act in a crisis. We hope they will anticipate our needs before we even realize we have them. It was true Grace and the most beautiful gift!

The song, *Hallelujah*, was a divine gift that I will cherish always. God played a song for me on the radio. That is Amazing Grace! God was faithful to me and did not forsake me. He drew me closer to Him through that experience and still draws me closer today. Hallelujah!

<u>Favorite Dad Memory:</u> My dad loved me.

Chapter 11

Review: What Just Happened?

When you are down in the valley,
that is where you are going to grow
because that is where the fertilizer is.

—Barbara Johnson

Week 1: Constipation.
Week 2: Prostate cancer suspected.
Week 3: Heart Attack—prostate cancer confirmed.
Week 4: Hospital discharge.
Week 5: Advanced stage prostate cancer confirmed
Week 6: Dad's lost hope. Kidney failure.
Week 7: End stage cancer confirmed. Palliative care.
Week 8: The miracle rally. Thanksgiving.
Week 9: Miracle fading.
Week 10: God welcomes Dad home. *Hallelujah.*

It was a whirlwind. It was difficult trying to make decisions and figure out what to do in an ever-changing landscape—it's hard to walk in shifting sand. It seemed like every few days or so, something else would happen and just when we thought we knew what we were dealing with, it had changed.

It felt like navigating through quick sand. The further you went, the deeper you sank and the more difficult it became. It felt as if we were slowly sinking with every effort to fight it, sinking us further. It felt like we could never get our bearings, every week brought a new challenge. There were always so many issues to address. It felt like trying to catch fish with your hands. There were many issues to try to grab a hold of. Once you caught one, you wanted to try to catch another but lost the first one. Just as you felt you were resolving something, it slipped away as another issue surfaced.

The irony was, the first day that Dad had gone to the hospital, the urologist suspected cancer and did a CT scan. The doctor told Dad and Brian the same day that he had cancer. Dad asked Brian not to say anything. Ooyyyy! I assume he didn't want to worry anyone, but I'm not sure why Dad wanted to keep that secret. I was flabbergasted that I didn't find this out until week five when Dad was in renal failure—it could have taken even longer, as it did for some family members, if I hadn't asked. It would have been far more effective health care if the doctor encouraged Dad to tell his family and provided resources and information. If you can look at a CT scan and see that, "the cancer is everywhere," then you should be smart enough to know that someone facing terminal illness should have support. The doctor knew that Dad was facing advanced stage or perhaps even end-stage cancer.

In a complex medical case, there seemed to be so many processes to manage—nurses, doctors, advocating for treatment, drug management, pain management, nutrition, Dad's needs, Mom's needs, communication between all of us (phone calls, emails, meetings), information, research, updates to family and friends, the conflicts and differences in opinion between us, the frustrations taken out on someone by mistake due to fear, stress, or battle fatigue. It seemed endless and continually challenging trying to figure out where we were and where we were going from here, if ever we knew where here really was.

As I look back, it never did feel like the issue of drugs and pain management was ever fully resolved to our satisfaction. And we never satisfactorily resolved the issue of bowel function which was the presenting problem in the first place. It seemed an endless cycle of distress and difficulty and questioning. It was definitely as slippery a fish that you could never get a firm grip on.

It felt like we couldn't save him even though somehow I thought maybe we could. How dualistic. I read books, I read online, I developed plans, I met with doctors – but it felt like anytime I felt like I could move forward, which wasn't often because I only had Dad's full cooperation on a few occasions, my efforts felt blocked and shut down. And it seemed like a spiritual block. There were many times when it felt like Dad was going to die . . . most of the time, in fact. It was hard to know what to pray for and even harder to know what to expect.

At one point, my friend Grace said, "I'm having trouble figuring out which horse to get on." Like my dad, I was praying for a quick healing or a quick death.

When we first received the cancer diagnosis and I started researching, I was hopeful that there were things we could try to help my dad fight the cancer cells that were invading his body. Through the last five weeks of Dad's life, I always had this enduring feeling that if I could just control my dad's diet, implement naturopathic, complementary therapies, and secure access to greater resources, that I could have helped Dad—maybe not cured but it felt like I could have helped Dad heal to some degree. I know that may sound unrealistic, especially to anyone who knows anything about advanced stage cancer with cancer cells metastasized to the bone. Once the cancer has spread that far, most doctors would not have any hope.

From the time I started to research prostate cancer on the internet and read the books I found at the library, I felt like there was some possibility for improvement in Dad's condition. I started to see cancer as the body's breakdown in the waste management system. I started to view cancer as an issue with not keeping up with taking out the trash. I started to see it like an issue of hoarding—something that's under control to a certain point and then just one or two conditions change and the whole house becomes filled with useless stuff and trash. It seemed to me that if you could get a strong enough clean-up going, then you could start to see improvement one small step at a time.

At this point I don't know if it was rational judgment based on my research, intuition or the Holy Spirit speaking to me, or just wishful thinking. Perhaps none of the above or perhaps all. Regardless, I really only had eleven days to implement any of my ideas toward improving the cancerous state in my Dad's body. On October 2, I was caught off guard and surprised when my dad was ready to start trying things and become my project. I was definitely unprepared and as a result, I couldn't really do very much. I couldn't completely control Dad's diet and I was not ready with experts and practitioners standing by ready to jump in and help—not that I would have had the cooperation of the doctors or the hospital. All of those things would have taken time, something that was in short supply.

I desperately wanted to know the truth from God about what was happening. And even though I realized from August 15 forward that Dad might die because this was, "going to be bad," I recognized that I had to hang on to hope and keep hanging on to hope over and over again. If I had known God's plan, I felt like I could have walked in the right direction. I would have done things differently if I had known from the outset that Dad had only eight weeks to live. And I would have been strong enough to cope with that, with God's Grace. I wouldn't have wasted so much time figuring out details about cancer, treatment, and options. I would have spent more time just be-ing with my dad. That's what the rest of the family seemed to be doing. At least I know we did everything we could and we left no stone unturned.

I realize still, how much I feel like I let my dad down. After Dad passed over to Heaven, every now and then when I was thinking of what we had been through, I would say out loud, "Oh, Dad" with sadness. I didn't think it was out of guilt. It seemed more out of sorrow for what had taken us by storm and Dad being separated from us. But now, I can see and feel that part of me felt I had failed in some ways. For sure, the issue of pain management felt like a failure. It always seemed to be a challenge. Also, the kidney was a red flag in the first week and should have been a warning for kidney failure. I missed the warning for kidney failure at least twice—it seems so obvious now but hindsight is twenty-twenty. The doctors didn't make the connection either—even more surprising. Also, my dad asked for Spiritual care on several occasions and it was in his Personal Directive as well. We never arranged any visits from clergy despite the fact that the minister from my church offered and that should have been a simple need to take care of. Those details can be haunting when you get in touch with them.

On the flipside, I was also amazed. As a family, in the end, I was amazed at how much support we were able to bring even if it was not perfect. I know, now that I have climbed that learning curve and could now support someone more effectively. Here's hoping I won't have to. I know Dad is in Heaven and despite those two months before he left earth being so difficult, he is absolutely fine now—far better than I can imagine I am sure.

Now that a year has passed, reading over all my notes and the emails sent out between family and friends, Dad's case looks really obvious. Even cut and dried. But at the time, it felt very scattered and like trying to put together a puzzle with pieces missing. Looking back, I see information that I missed. As I read all of Robert's updates, there was a lot of key information that I didn't really see. I think that when doctors give information to patients and their families, they probably need to repeat it at least two or three times. I noticed for myself that it always took some time for information to sink in. And if there was any information that didn't fit what the doctors told you, it was easy to start questioning what was happening and begin looking for other solutions. I wish I had spent some time just going over the information we had from the beginning—that would have helped me understand the diagnosis earlier. I would have figured out the kidney failure earlier as well. I would have understood the bowel issue and the paralytic ileus sooner. Of course, it would have been much more helpful to have the diagnosis upfront with a referral to an oncologist who could have briefed us on what to expect and what to look for. That would have been really helpful. But we didn't. And I didn't. Perhaps the outcome still would have, "been bad."

As far as people and personal strength go, I would have to say that I'm not that strong of a person. My life has been relatively easy. It is through adversity and challenging times that we grow stronger and develop our ability to cope in difficult times. Prior to my dad's illness I would have said that going through this kind of adversity would have crushed me and I never would have had the strength to cope. In fact, I have often joked that I could be on the verge of a nervous breakdown if I discover I have run out of milk or raisin bran. Although not entirely true it is a recognition of the life stage I have been in for the past ten or fifteen years, my standing on the precipice of burnout in 2001, my less than stellar adrenal glands, my lack of resiliency, and my lack of ability to cope with either mountains or mole hills.

It was such a surprise to find out that God would carry me through the entire experience—carrying me in His Grace every step of the way. This was easily the most difficult season in my life but God made it so much lighter and easier than I ever could have imagined He could. That was the power of God's Grace! Hallelujah.

In my experience with the toughest season of my life, I experienced an outpouring of God's love into my heart. I felt so blessed because I didn't even have to ask God to walk with me. It felt like He was just there walking with me, sometimes even carrying me. I didn't have to reach out my hand to God for Him to take it. As soon as I moved my hand, I realized God's hand was already there reaching out to me before I even knew I would need to grab it. It was a dual, dichotomous experience: it was hard and painful but I was buffered. It was as if I lived in a bubble of God's Grace, wrapped around me, protecting me, propping me up so I wouldn't fall. I discovered firsthand that God really is great at shining light into dark places. Hallelujah!

<u>Favorite Dad Memory:</u> When I was fourteen, I was upset about something and I went into my room and lay on my bed crying. My dad came in and just sat on the edge of my bed and started rubbing my back to console me. He didn't say anything, he was just there. Then he left. I felt comforted. When I was older, I realized how wonderful it was of my dad to just be there with me when I was upset and not tell me how to feel or how not to feel or change my reaction in any way. He was just there for comfort to let me ride out the feeling and let it go.

Lesson: Sometimes the only thing you can do is "just be there" and sometimes the best thing you can do is "just be there."

Chapter 12

The Funeral and Memorial

The family met at Mom's house the day after Dad passed away to decide how to proceed. Dad had a file on his computer, a very lengthy file that detailed his wishes and personal information titled: "Instructions re: Emergencies or Death of John W. Bennett." The first of the nine pages consisted of twenty-seven guidelines for carrying out his last wishes.

Dad didn't want a funeral per se, but he was okay with a memorial service, for the sake of the living, so we decided we would plan a service in celebration of Dad's life—a life definitely well lived. Mom also wanted to hold a family-only service within the next few days so we decided we would do that for her. Katherine handled most of the arrangements for the small service, and we divided up the responsibilities for the memorial. Dad's instructions stated that the Scripture at his service was "to be selected by daughters Katherine and Wendy." I chose Revelations 21:6-7 and Isaiah 40:31 and decided to share my experience of being with Dad in his last days.

On Wednesday, October 27, 2010, I spoke at the family service:

> *He said to me, "It is done. I am the Alpha and the Omega, the Beginning and the End. To him who is thirsty I will give to drink without cost from the spring of the water of life. He who overcomes will inherit all of this, and I will be his God and he will be my son.*
>
> Rev 21: 6-7 (NIV)

> *But those who hope in the Lord will renew their strength. They will soar on wings like eagles; they will run and not grow weary, they will walk and not be faint.*
>
> Isaiah 40:31

<u>My Dad</u>: *Grace, Harmony, Love*

On Wednesday a week ago it became apparent that Dad was nearing the end of his life. He had told Katherine that he needed to go and wanted to die. On Thursday and Friday I visited Dad during the daytime and spent some time alone with him.

I described how I anointed Dad with the communion oil and baptized him with the Holy water from the Jordan River. I talked about how I wrote the words Grace, Harmony, and Love on his abdomen because that was my wish for him in his body and on his journey—and how I realized that that was what my dad was for me.

I shared the words that I whispered in Dad's ear about love, his gifts, lessons, God, permission to leave his body, going to Heaven, how God would welcome him home—knowing that soon God would have Dad with him and we would be the ones missing him . . . Until we meet again.

I also said: *Now I can whisper to him anytime and anywhere, whenever I feel like it: Dad there will always be a space in our family where you once lived in your earthly body. Sometimes it will seem like an empty space or a huge gap that looks like the Grand Canyon. And other times it will seem like a space that you still fill—even from where you are now—infused with Grace, love, and harmony. Thank you for everything!*

The Memorial

We held the memorial service about a month after Dad's passing. We knew it would take on a bit of a show quality because of his involvement in so many musical groups, and we wanted a celebration, as did he. Dad may have been an engineer with an MBA from Cornell University, but music had always been a very important part of his life, especially after retirement. He grew up in a musical family; he played French horn for the Montreal Junior Symphony; he played piano; he joined Barbershoppers in 1972; he was in a quartet for almost thirty years; he attended Harmony College on several occasions; he became a chorus director; he coached every chorus in Calgary and travelled around coaching quartets and choruses in many different places; he was inducted into the Barbershop Hall of Fame; he joined the Master's Singers Chorus; he joined the Westside Singers—a Christian mixed choir (both men and women); and he taught ukulele classes to children and seniors.

Mom and Dad had grown up in the United Church, but when they moved to Calgary from Montreal in 1963, they stopped attending as regularly. They both seemed to find their fellowship, community, and Grace in their music.

Five of Dad's twenty-seven instructions in his file were as follows:

1. Minimize costs
2. Music—live, upbeat gospel singing, live barbershop, if possible
3. Music, Scripture, and Clergy Selections—to be selected by daughters Katherine and Wendy
4. Sing, dance, laugh, and celebrate
5. Eulogy—keep it short

The tone of the Memorial had been set, and we were fairly certain, or at least hopeful, that many of Dad's musical groups would be willing to participate. We decided to hold it at the church Michael and I attended with our minister presiding. Mom wanted Dad's brother and Brian to give eulogies. Dad's friend and colleague asked Mom if he could speak as well. She said yes, so he and his wife planned to fly back from Palm Springs to attend and give a eulogy. As planning progressed, we lined up: two Christian choral groups, four Barbershop choruses, two Sweet Adeline choruses, two quartets, and three eulogies. Brian also wanted to sing and play Dad's ukulele, and his son Mark wanted to sing and play a song he had written on the guitar. Katherine asked me if I would like to sing "The Lord's Prayer" with her, accompanied by Brian and Katherine on guitar, and even though the thought was very intimidating, I decided I would do it.

At this point I was thinking that I should consider choreographing a dance to "Hallelujah" by Heather Williams, but I wasn't sure. When I asked Mom about it, she said it would be fine, and the rest of the family agreed. Brian said it would fulfill the aspect of dance in Dad's last wishes. I wasn't sure how it would be received though. I went back and forth in my mind many times. Dad's wish was for us to "sing, laugh dance, and celebrate," and I felt that I wanted to dance and that God wanted me to as well, so I finally decided I would do it. I also decided to share my "Hallelujah" story.

That cold, stormy day, November 21, 2010, nearly five hundred people came out to help us pay tribute to and celebrate the life of John Bennett.

After singing the Lord's Prayer, and just before performing my dance, I spoke:

Memorial Service—Dad's "Hallelujah"

The story of this dance is a little long. I will try to convey the meaning of it for me as briefly as possible since I'm not really supposed to speak.

I told the story of how we took Dad back to the hospital on September 23 in renal failure and the difficult week that followed when Dad had no will to live. I described my experience of hearing "Hallelujah" on the radio and being comforted by God's Grace. I shared how God seemed to be playing that song for me leading up to the miraculous Friday night by my dad's bedside. I read the definition of the word miracle and explained how Dad's spirit seemed healed and re-enlivened, and his hope had been restored. I tried to impart the true Grace of those moments and how unbelievable it all seemed. I read the email that Brian wrote to us the next day when he saw the change in Dad. I described how I found out the song was by Heather Williams and how God played it for me ten days later in my car.

I continued speaking: *So this is for you, Dad—for the Grace and Harmony and Love with which you lived your life and loved your family and friends, and your God. And this is for you, God, for all the gifts you give all of us, the Love and Care you have for each of us, and the Grace you continually bestow upon us. Can I get a Hallelujah, Amen from you?*

"Hallelujah, Amen!" the memorial attendees answered me.

"Amen!"

And as I'm dancing and you see me on the floor, if you could just say a quick little prayer for me to get up. I'm about a hundred years old in dancer's years.

Participating so fully in the service was very healing. I loved the memorial, and it almost felt as if Dad were there with us—I'm sure he was there in spirit. Thinking about it the next day, however, I felt I had not been well received, and coping with that much vulnerability has always been challenging for me. Still, no matter what anyone else had thought, I felt good about my offering to God and Dad.

One of the Barbershop choruses sang "Turn Your Radio On" during the service, and in his speech, the director referred to my story about "Hallelujah." I had heard the chorus sing this song many, many times growing up, but I didn't realize how spiritual the lyrics are until I heard them sung at the memorial. It was written by Albert E. Brumley in 1938 (he also wrote "I'll Fly Away,"—one of Dad's favorite hymns which everyone sang at the memorial too). This song was my experience both in reality and as a metaphor. What God wants us to know is that it can be everyone's experience: listen, and get in touch with God! "Well come and listen into a radio station where the mighty hosts of heaven sing . . . If you wanna feel those good vibrations coming from the joy that His love can bring . . . Turn your radio on and listen to the music in the air—and glory, glory share. Get in touch with God. Turn your radio on. A don't you know that everybody is a radio receiver, all you gotta do is listen for the call. If you listen in you will be a believer leanin' on the truth that will never fall."

In Brian's first email regarding Dad's illness sent on August 25, he signed off with "Stay Tuned." It turns out that is fabulous advice. Stay tuned because The Holy Spirit is talking to us and will guide us if we work on how to listen!

The memorial service was brilliant, and I believe Dad would have been pleased. In fact, I'm sure he was. We had hoped to keep it to two hours, but it turned out to be nearly three. So much for "keep it short"—I'm sure Dad thought it was too long.

We celebrated Dad's life in a fantastic way, and it was so uplifting. I wasn't sad that day. I felt happy that Dad had led a life well lived and had been well loved and I was grateful that he had been my dad.

On the back of the program was a scripture verse:

> *Make a joyful noise unto the LORD, all ye lands.*
>
> *Serve the LORD with gladness; come before His presence with singing.*
>
> *Know ye that the LORD he is God; it is He that hath made us, and not we ourselves; we are his people, and the sheep of his pasture.*
>
> *Enter into his gates with thanksgiving, and into his courts with praise; be thankful unto Him, and bless His name.*
>
> *For the LORD is good; His mercy is everlasting; and His truth endureth to all generations.*

—*Psalm 100: 1-5 (KJV)*

Favorite Dad Memory: Four or five years ago, I was over at Mom and Dad's for dinner and was in the kitchen with Dad and a few other family members. I made a comment about not being a very good cook especially considering I was married with four children. Dad said to me, "Well Wendy, you can't be good at everything!" This was one of the nicest compliments I had received in quite a while and it stayed with me for a long time. I can usually ride a month or two on a lovely compliment! Dad was good at making people feel good—when he said something complementary about someone, he meant it.

Lesson: It is nice to reflect the good qualities of people back to them so they know that you think highly of them. Nowhere is this more profound than during a celebration of life and the memorialization of a loved one.

Chapter 13

Year of Mourning: My Experiences with an Invisible Dad

Be still and know that I am God.

—Psalm 46:10

*We are meant to listen more than we talk. That is why
God gave us two ears and only one mouth.*

—Unknown

They say (the elusive "they") that if you lose someone close
to you, someone you love, someone from your inner
circle, then you have an angel in Heaven. And I am sure
that I do.

When you are in a close relationship with someone on Earth
such as a spouse, parent, or close friend, you can become closer
to that person, as well as to God, when you both have a faith. You
become three points on a triangle—moving closer to one point can
move you closer to the other point in the triangle. And I believe

you can still experience this God triangle with a person in Heaven as well. It seems my dad's closeness to God has brought me closer as well.

After my father's illness and passing and everything that I experienced, I found that my tolerance for anything dark became much lower and my need for all things light much greater. I think this is a natural evolution in our spiritual journey, as our capacity to experience Grace, increases. I had never liked watching violent shows or movies but at this point, I almost could not stand to see what would be considered mild or moderate levels of violence, profanity, or crass sexuality, and I craved shows that were uplifting and enlightening. I attributed this to being so close to the portal of Heaven through my dad's passing and the Grace that seemed to surround me.

With my intolerance for darkness and craving for all things light and of God, I have changed what television I watch, books I read, and music I listen to. I pray more frequently and more regularly. But most of all, I feel like I am closer to God and walking more closely with Jesus and the Holy Spirit.

In the book *Infinite Quest*, John Edward suggests that we should journal with loved ones who have passed over and learn to listen and be still. He also suggests that death is like going deaf. The old language isn't available, so you need to learn a new language to communicate. Death is viewed as a transition in a relationship, not an end or a hiatus.

In December and January, I was doing laundry in the laundry room of our home and the lights began to flicker. It seemed to happen regularly while I was in there over the course of a month or so. I wondered if it was Dad trying to get my attention. I had read before that people who have had a close loved one die can experience strange things with electricity, such as lights flickering on and off. Intriguing . . .

<u>Until We Meet Again . . . Special Dispensation</u>

In early January of 2011, I was watching an episode of *Touched by An Angel* on DVD titled, "Till We Meet Again." As soon as I saw the title, the episode grabbed my attention—I had said to Dad, "I will miss you . . . until we meet again." It was about a man who was dying. His three adult children came home to be with him. The man, Joe Carpenter (a symbol for Jesus' earthly father, Joseph, who was a carpenter?), tried to tell his youngest daughter the family secret—a secret that he had kept for many years. Joe wanted her to know that she was not his biological child but the result of her mother's affair with his business partner. But then Joe had a stroke and could not speak. The angel, Monica, asked God for a special dispensation, and God answered yes. Then the daughter found out the truth from her mother, and was greatly distressed. God re-enlivened Joe, and he walked downstairs and began to play the piano. He played a song the family used to sing together in four-part harmony—like barbershop. The family heals by making peace with the truth with the knowledge that they all loved and cared about each other. Then Joe's wife and kids sing "Till We Meet Again" as Joe passes and goes home to Heaven with the Angel of Death, Andrew.

Some of the lyrics from "Till We Meet Again" (written in 1918 by Raymond B. Egan and Richard Whiting) are:

> *Over high garden walls this sweet echo falls*
> *As a soldier boy whispers goodbye*
> *Smile the while you kiss me sad adieu*
> *When the clouds roll by I'll come to you*
> *Then the skies will seem more blue . . .*
> *Every tear will be a memory*
> *So wait and pray each night for me*
> *Until we meet again.*

I said goodbye to my dad but we will only be apart for a while—until we meet again. As I watched this episode, I was riveted. I saw so many parallels to my story, and it felt like confirmation of what I had experienced. Our family didn't receive the big miracle of healing that I kept thinking God might give Dad but we did receive many gifts of Grace through the process. And I thought we received a "special dispensation" just like Joe Carpenter—I received the song "Hallelujah" playing on the radio which led up to the Friday night when my dad's spirit seemed so re-enlivened and healed. Hallelujah!

The Book Idea

> *Endurance is not just the ability to bear a hard thing, but to turn it into glory.*
>
> —William Barclay

I don't know how the idea came to me exactly. I saw a scripture from the book of Isaiah while I was watching *Full Circle* or *100 Huntley Street* when it dawned on me: I should write a book and call it *"Hallelujah."* Michael had given me a white journal for Christmas—the white symbolized God's light to me. On the front cover was a quote by Alfred de Souza:

> *Dance as though no one is watching you*
> *Love as though you have never been hurt before*
> *Sing as though no one can hear you*
> *Live as though heaven is on earth*

I made an entry in my God journal that read:

> *January 17, 2011: Write a book about my experience with Dad and God. Title: "Hallelujah"*

Isaiah 43: 2-3 (RSV): . . . when you walk through the fire,
you shall not be burned, and the flame shall not consume you.
For I am the Lord your God . . .

When I wrote that, it felt like the book was God's idea and the voice of the Holy Spirit was guiding me. The scripture encapsulated my experience with God and my dad's passing. God carried me through that season and I praise Him for it because otherwise, I wouldn't have made it—at least not so unscathed. I walked through the fire and it did not consume me . . . because of God's Grace. Hallelujah!

God's Message: Trust and Fear Not

Throughout January and February, the words "trust" and "fear not" were prominent on my radar. I kept noticing these themes in scripture, songs, radio and television discussions, as well as in my own prayer and meditation. It felt as if God was preparing me. "Trust Me" has always been something God has asked me to do—something He calls us all to do. The words are in the bedrock scripture of my personal faith journey:

Trust in the Lord with all your heart and lean not onto your
own understanding. In all your ways, acknowledge Him and
he will direct your path.
—Proverbs 3: 5-6 (HNV)

Recently on *Full Circle,* one of the hosts asked, "What is the most frequent command of the New Testament?" I thought to myself, it must be "fear not." I was right. I knew the answer because God had focused me early in 2011 and I was getting the message. Living it, of course, is another thing. If we do trust in God, with all our heart, and we are not afraid, then anything truly is possible. The more we trust and the less we fear, the closer we can walk with our Lord.

I wondered, at the time, why God was telling me this, since I had just had such an amazing experience with God through the time of my dad's illness, passing, and memorial. I thought that perhaps it was due to the disconcerted feelings I had after singing, speaking, and dancing at Dad's memorial. I felt that I should have been more cautious and less exposed, and that feeling still lingers today. It is rooted in the fear of being judged or deemed crazy, but as I said in my email to family and friends on October 4 (my mini-Easter experience and special dispensation):

> . . . *I normally am quite careful about what I tell most people about my experiences of God because some people don't have the ears to hear or the eyes to see and just assume you are crazy. In this case, I say, think whatever you like because I am crazy . . . crazy about JESUS!!!!!! There it is . . . AMEN.*

I had been fearless the day I sent that email and fearless at my dad's memorial, but fear still creeps in every now and then. I believe God is working on me to change this. Fear separates us from God and trust brings us closer, just as it does in our other relationships. I think that God wants me to trust Him and fear not so that I can be prepared for what I will face in the future, whatever that may be.

Scripture in Philippians 4:6-7 (NIV) has also come up in my life several times:

> *Do not be anxious about anything, but in everything, by prayer and petition, with Thanksgiving, present your requests to God. And the peace of God, which transcends all understanding will guard your hearts and minds in Christ Jesus.*

I wrote this scripture on the first page of my new God journal underneath the acronym TRUST which I saw on *Full Circle*:

Take one day at a time!   *Matthew 6:34*
Remember all things work together for good.   *Romans 8:28*
Under no circumstances worry.   *Philippians 4:6*
Start every day with prayer and Thanksgiving. *1 Thes 5:16-18*
The Lord will never forsake you.   *Hebrews 13:5*

Dreams

I have had prophetic dreams before—dreams that I believe are from God. In fact, I believe that if you pray for something or ask God a question before you go to sleep, God may answer you in a dream—that's how we "sleep on it." Many Christians believe that God can communicate with us in our dreams. The problem for many of us, including me, is that we often don't remember our dreams, especially if we are sleep-deprived or hormonally challenged. When I have a very lucid dream, I try to write it down first thing in the morning while it is still fresh in my mind.

In February, I had a dream about my dad:

> *I was at my mom and dad's house sitting in the living room. Suddenly I noticed Dad was walking across the room—he just sort of appeared. I jumped up and hugged him with surprise, shock, and elation. I asked him if he was really alive and he said yes. He looked healthy and strong, happy and calm. I asked him what had happened and he laughed. Then Katherine came and I told her, "Look, it's Dad! He's alive! We've got to call Mom and tell her." But we didn't know Mom's number. Robert was there too. Then the doorbell rang. It was Brian. I told him, "You're not going to believe it!" We were so happy and so surprised. I said to Dad, "But you died . . . are you dead or alive? Is it like a near-death experience?" Dad said, "Yes I died but now I'm back and I'm fine. It's like a near-death experience. It's unbelievable." I wanted to ask him about it and hear every detail. I said, "But we cremated your body. How did you get it back?" He*

said, "There was just enough of a DNA strand to recreate it." Then Mom came home. I said, "Mom, Mom, you're not going to believe it. Dad's back and he's alive." Mom looked so happy and was laughing as she sat down on the couch beside him.

I wasn't entirely sure what this dream meant. I first interpreted it to mean that my dad was alive in Heaven and was trying to tell me he was still with me. The dream could also be a reflection of my wish that Dad was still alive on Earth. The nature of the dream reminded me of Lazarus, coming back from the dead. I didn't think this was what God was trying to tell me, but I wasn't sure.

In April I had another dream about my dad:

Dad was driving in what appeared to be his new car. I think it was a red convertible. He was driving down a highway on a beautiful day. Dad had called me on his cell phone. We hung up and then I realized that Dad was alive, so I called him back. Then I realized his voice sounded different and he might be sick still or sick again. Dad said he was worried about that too so we started talking about the cancer and what he should do. He was alive. Michael and I were so shocked, surprised, and happy.

In the dream, Dad looked healthy. He was driving a shiny, new car, unlike any he had driven while he was alive, in a beautiful, vibrant place that I didn't recognize. Both dreams were so strong and so vivid that I can still see the images in my mind, eight months later.

As I thought about this dream, I wondered if God was fine-tuning His message for me. Instead of Dad sitting on the couch and speaking to us face-to-face, he was travelling somewhere far away that I didn't recognize. Dad could contact me via cell phone and I could contact him, but it seemed much more remote somehow. I felt more convinced that Dad was "alive." He is further away, but he is alive and I can still communicate with him somehow. I wish

I did have a cell phone I could call up to Heaven with. That would be fabulous!

Arianna's Question

In May 2011, Arianna asked me at dinner one evening, "How come Granddaddy had to die?"

I replied, "That's a very big question and it's hard to know for sure. The physical earthly answer is that the cancer was discovered too late and there was nothing we could do and the cancer killed him. The spiritual, Godly answer is that it was Granddaddy's time to die and go home to God and that's what he did."

"I wish he didn't have to die!"

"Me too!" I replied.

Arianna has said more recently that she would like to be the first one to read my book.

Reminder

On Friday, June 10, I had another incredible experience. "Incredible" is an interesting word. To me, it means something really great or amazing but it also means something so great that it's not credible:

1. too extraordinary or improbable to be believed;
2. amazing, extraordinary.

But I digress.

I had been reading the book *The Boy Who Came Back from Heaven* and enjoying it immensely. I love the Malarkey family's story of their journey with their son's near-death/went-to-Heaven-to-be-with-Jesus-and-came-back-to-Earth-again experience. It is extremely powerful and inspiring, to say the least.

Kevin Malarkey and his six year old son, Alex, were in a horrific car accident that left Alex paralyzed and in a coma for two months. Beth, Alex's mother, had unfailing faith from the time she first found out about the accident that nearly killed her son, through Alex's recovery, to the present day. She held to the single-minded belief that her son would survive and be healed. I started to wonder, *Was I faithful enough? Or in the right way? If I had been more faithful, would my dad still be alive today?* At the time when Dad was ill, I felt like I had absolute faith in God's plan even though I didn't know what that plan was. I prayed for my dad's healing, yet I seemed to know that God had a different plan. As I read this lovely book about Heaven, I asked God, *Should I have had more faith in Dad's healing from cancer? Would that have changed the outcome?* These thoughts left me feeling sad and wishing I had walked through the experience of my dad's disease differently.

Michael and I were in the middle of a large renovation project at our rental condo. That night, around ten o'clock, we went over to the condo and started working. I usually put on a CD, since music always relaxes me and makes anything, even painting, more fun. But the CD wouldn't play which had never happened before. I switched to the radio, Shine FM, and it worked. I tried the CD again but it still didn't play so I decided to *turn the radio on.*

About five minutes later, "Hallelujah" began to play. So lovely and delightful! I had only heard my song (or "Our" song) once or twice since the day Dad passed over to Heaven, despite the fact that I had been listening to Shine FM almost exclusively. I had mentioned to God last December that anytime he wanted to get my attention, He could play our song on the radio . . . if He wanted. I wondered, *Is God trying to tell me something?* Then five or ten minutes later, "Out of my Hands" began playing. Wow! Another fifteen or twenty minutes later, a radio interview began, and a man started talking about his father's memorial which had been held in

January. He discussed how it is easier coping with the death of a loved one when you know the person who passed knew and loved God and Jesus. Then he said, "I know this is strange to say, but my dad's memorial was a blast." Incredible!

The fact that his father had passed would have been more than enough to get my attention, but the memorial being a blast? I could completely relate and had said similar things myself about my dad's memorial service—because it was a blast! At that point, I was tuned in and my attention was piqued. As I listened, I thought, *God is speaking to me*. Hallelujah!

God was answering my question and reminding me that it had been Dad's time and there was nothing I could have done. It was out of my hands—it was from the start. My faith had always been one hundred percent. I hadn't known what God's plan was, but I had had absolute faith that God had a plan and it would come to fruition.

In the movie, *Oh, God!* God says to Jerry Landers (played by John Denver), "You have the kind of faith that comes from knowing." Since I first began to really know God, I have felt that I have been blessed with *that kind of faith*. But Jesus's words "By your own faith, you are healed" can plague you if you believe you could have done something differently by prayer, thought, faith, or action.

> *Then Jesus told them, "I assure you, if you have faith and don't doubt, you can do things like this and much more. You can even say to this mountain, "May God lift you up and throw you into the sea," and it will happen. If you believe, you will receive whatever you ask for in prayer."*

—Matthew 21:21-22 (NLT)

Well, cancer was my mountain and I was not able to throw it into the sea, but I believed it was possible, right up until the end. In the end, it was up to God. I was aware of this when my dad was ill and lay dying. Looking back, I can see that all my efforts to help my dad get better were eventually blocked or never got off the ground.

It became clear to me that night that God was reassuring me and re-minding me—with the songs "Hallelujah" and "Out of My Hands" as well as the man being interviewed about his father's passing and wonderful memorial. It was not about my lack of faith. It was about God's will and Dad's time. Hallelujah!

I later read a passage from "Conversations with God" by Neale Donald Walsch which reassured me even more. Neale asks God:

> *What about the person who is sick, but has the faith that will move mountains – and so thinks, says, and believes he's going to get better. . . only to die six weeks later?*

And God replies:

> *The person who has the "faith to move mountains," and dies six weeks later, has moved mountains for six weeks. That may have been enough for him. He may have decided, on the last hour of the last day, "Okay, I've had enough. I'm ready to go on to another adventure." You may not have known of that decision because he may not have told you.*

So perhaps our faith did move mountains.

The CD player worked fine after that—no further problems.

Summer

In July 2011, I was listening to someone speak about the importance of praying and spending time with God every day: "Be still and know that I am God." This is such a familiar theme in my life now. I have heard this scripture several times before, of course, but have never really lived it as fully as I would like. In fact, many years ago I often thought, *I have this wonderful faith and yet forget to use it a great deal of the time.* I have heard before that Mother Teresa and Martin Luther King, Jr. used to wake up between four and five o'clock each day to pray for two or three hours. Wow!

I am fond of saying, "I have never been a morning person. Before I had children, I was a night person. Now, I'm not anything." Knowing this, I said to God, "if you want me to pray at the beginning of the day, then you might want to wake me up early. I'll never be able to do it on my own." Since then, God has been waking me up early, almost every morning like clockwork—usually twenty minutes before my alarm goes off and sometimes up to an hour before. Hallelujah.

In the past year, and through my grief, I had grown closer to God and was living "in the light" more than ever. Lights had flickered on and off. I missed my dad but I had true joy in my heart because I knew I would be okay, "Until we meet again" as the *Touched by An Angel* episode affirmed for me. In fact, I felt Dad was still with me in Spirit. God inspired me to write a manuscript or a blog to tell my story and God reminded me many times to "Trust" and "Fear not." I felt Dad had visited me in my dreams. I felt God had communicated with me through the radio again to reassure me about the truth of my experience and my faith. God was waking me up early each day "to be still and know" and begin the day hangin' out with my sweet Lord. I was so grateful for the comfort of God's Grace. Hallelujah!

Favorite Dad Memory: Dad was teaching ukulele to kids in a grade three or four class in an area that tended to have fewer resources than most schools in Calgary. One little boy was struggling to learn the chords and told my dad that he could play only one chord. My dad told him, "That's fine. You play that one chord with all your gusto. Watch me directing and I'll point to you when you should play your chord." Dad would cue him so the little boy would know when to chime in.

Lesson: Everyone can participate, and everyone has something to bring or to add. No one should be left out. We all add our own notes to the harmony of life in the symphony we all create together. Even when it seems like we can't do what is required, we can always do just what we can—nothing is too insignificant.

Chapter 14

Dragonflies

Where there is an open mind there will always be a frontier.

—Charles Kettering

I t is completely amazing how events sometimes unfold. As you journey with God, incredible things can happen—things that make you think to yourself, *If I tell anyone what has happened, they will think I have lost my mind and gone around the proverbial bend.* And yet, you know them to be the truth and that these things are real.

There is a quotation from the movie *Babe* I have always liked because it reminds me of how our God, a God of wonder, is able to work through us:

> *When the thoughts first came to him, Farmer Hoggett dismissed it as mere whimsy, but like most of his hair-brained ideas, it wouldn't go away . . . But Farmer Hoggett knew that little ideas . . . that tickled and nagged and refused to go away . . . should never be ignored . . . for in them lie the seeds of destiny.*

One of the many themes in this lovely film about a small pig with an unprejudiced heart, is that sometimes you have to take a leap of faith and follow your intuition, instincts, or the still, small voice within and follow your heart. Some people believe that the still, small voice within is God's voice inside you—I know I do. It is the Holy Spirit, abiding within.

In July 2011, I kept seeing dragonflies. This is not an unusual occurrence in the summertime in Canada, but there seemed to be more than normal and unusual enough to catch my attention. Then in early August, over three days, I found a dead dragonfly each day and I began to wonder if there was something symbolic about these interesting insects and my dad's passing. It may seem like an odd connection to make, but their appearances began shortly before the anniversary of my dad's illness. I wondered about this briefly, but didn't make too much of it and moved on.

I knew that as August 15 approached and all of the significant dates following, I would think of my dad and family and everything we had experienced the year before. Susan A. Berger, in her book, *The Five Ways We Grieve,* outlines five types of grievers. I am a "memorialist" when it comes to grieving, and so I knew I would find marking the anniversaries comforting in some ways and that I would want to take the time to reflect and think about my dad and how much I missed him.

On August 20, 2011, Michael and I and Arianna and Andrew took a trip to Lake Windermere in British Columbia. We were staying a week at a condo in Invermere, very close to the lake. On a whim, we had bid on and won the trip in a silent auction at the fundraising gala we had attended on September 25, when my dad was in the hospital.

The first day, as we were driving to the tennis courts in town, I noticed a deer grazing by a fence. As we were playing tennis, I noticed an eagle flying overhead. This is unusual because those who know me quite well know that, I am never the first person to see anything! I was always the child in the car on road trips who always seemed to miss whatever my mom pointed out along the road. Michael, on the other hand, has the eyes of a hawk and always notices everything, well ahead of me. I was struck by these animals and felt that they were signs for me, especially the eagle, which is considered to be a very spiritual animal in Aboriginal culture. The eagle is a symbol of spirit, vision, and strength, and the deer is a symbol of gentleness, unconditional love, and kindness.

I also noticed the abundance of dragonflies in the area. I recalled the dragonflies at home and remembered that my favorite skirt has two dragonflies embroidered on the back. Later on (in September) I noticed that my skirt has a larger and a smaller dragonfly, like a parent and a child. Interesting.

In his book *Inspiration: Your Ultimate Calling*, Dr. Wayne Dyer includes an anecdote about a butterfly landing on his hand. Dr. Dyer describes what a spiritual experience it had been and how privileged he had felt. My dad and I used to talk about Wayne Dyer and we both enjoyed his lectures on PBS. In fact, it was my dad who gave me Dr. Dyer's book and matching inspiration cards for Christmas. I had taken these cards to Dad's hospital room to use for visualization after the special dispensation miracle of October 1, 2010.

I said to my dad and God, "If this is your doing and these dragonflies are somehow connected to you, then have a dragonfly land on me." I told Michael about my thoughts and my request to God and Dad.

The next morning, while we were having breakfast out on the balcony, a dragonfly landed on my hand but I flinched before realizing what it was and it flew away. I was inspired. Not once in my life had a dragonfly ever landed on me. And certainly not after asking God and my dad to make it happen.

Then, a few minutes later, a dragonfly landed on my shoulder and Michael noticed it. He went to get his BlackBerry and came back out and took a few pictures. The dragonfly just sat on my shoulder for a few minutes while I tried not to make any sudden movements. I was in awe. I was excited. I found it unbelievable, but I believed it. *Would anyone else?* I wondered. I was so happy that I had told Michael about my thoughts before the dragonfly landed. It was definitely a more powerful experience for both of us because we had discussed it beforehand. He was also a bit shocked and surprised and full of wonder. Hallelujah!

While playing tennis later that morning, I wondered, *Was that really a spiritual experience or merely a random coincidence?* Just then a dragonfly flew right in front of me, as if to confirm the truth. Later in the day, I saw three eagles flying above the lake not far from the condo. I wondered if there was a nest close by. Perhaps the eagles regularly made an appearance, but it still seemed mystical somehow.

The following morning, while I was out on the condo balcony after breakfast, a dragonfly landed on my leg and stayed there for a minute or two. I gently reached over and picked up my camera, but when I turned the power on and the shutter released, it flew up to the wind chime. I managed to snap a few shots before it flew off. Wow—again! Incredible . . . yet credible.

The next morning, Michael saw three dragonflies lined up outside the window. When I woke up he said to me, "The dragonflies are out there waiting for you." We laughed. Later that morning, we went to play tennis, and Arianna drew a dragonfly, a heart, and my dad's name, John, on the side of the court with chalk. Michael took a photo. Clearly, this was having an impact on Arianna as well.

At the beach, a day and a half later, we were swimming out over our heads when a dragonfly landed on my head just by my forehead and hairline and stayed there for several minutes. I was completely in awe—these experiences coincided with the anniversaries of my dad's illness.

Later that afternoon, Michael and I realized his BlackBerry had become damp while inside a compartment of the Seadoo we rented and it was totally dead. We were worried it was destroyed, and couldn't figure out how it had been exposed to the dampness. We had placed it in a sealed plastic bag inside a water-tight compartment in the front part of the seat. Michael removed the battery and dried it out in the sun. A few hours later, he put the battery back in and then much later, around midnight, the power finally came back on. It still worked, but he had lost all his photos, videos, and music, as well as several other files. We were both disappointed because we had lost the photos of the dragonfly on my shoulder. Michael said he would ask someone in his IT department at work if there was a way to recover his files. It was a sad moment—we had lost part of the proof of my experience. Also we had thought, somewhat fancifully, about putting the dragonfly picture on the book cover if, in fact, I did decide to write a book and if, in fact, it was published.

The next day, a dragonfly landed on my God journal which was on the stool beside my chair. I had been carrying the journal around with me so I could write about my remarkable experiences while the details were fresh in my mind. And then later, while we were swimming, another dragonfly landed on my head. I told Michael I was considering asking some of the locals if there were always so many dragonflies around, and if they landed on people often. Michael told me, with complete resolve, "No, it's you!" Interestingly, after that conversation, I saw very few dragonflies around me, but when I observed the lack of dragonflies and started thinking about it, the dragonflies started coming around again. Intriguing.

From the time the first dragonfly landed on me, I didn't doubt the meaning or significance of the experience. However, the logical thinker in me wanted to keep from jumping to unwarranted conclusions. The evidence was compelling though, to say the least.

While considering this incredible experience I was having with the myriad of dragonflies, the Disney movie *Mulan* came to mind. *Mulan* is the story of a young Chinese woman who sneaks off to join the army so her father won't have to. She disguises herself as a man to save her father's life. Three aspects of the movie seemed salient as I thought about it. First, Mulan's ancestors watch over the family from the other side. Was Dad watching over me from Heaven? Second, Mulan's grandmother gives her a cricket that she considers lucky and it stays with Mulan throughout the story. Third, Mulan tries to save her father's life by joining the army in her father's place. I told Michael how I was thinking about the parallels of *Mulan* to my experience and Michael joked, "Maybe my grandmother [who passed over to Heaven in 1996] will send me a wasp and it will sting me." We laughed. About twenty minutes later, a wasp, seemingly out of nowhere, flew up to Michael and stung him. What? Unbelievable! Seriously . . .

Back in Calgary, Michael took his BlackBerry to his IT department at work, but was told nothing could be done. The photos, videos, music, and other files were gone. Disappointment.

On the morning of Thursday, September 1, I heard *Hallelujah* on the car radio while I was out running errands. I wondered if God was trying to get my attention. Then that afternoon, I was sitting outside on the deck in our backyard mulling over a stressful decision I needed to make regarding my dad's estate when a dragonfly landed on my foot and stayed there for about thirty seconds. I almost flinched but quickly realized it was a dragonfly, and it stayed. It appeared that Dad and God were with me, and they definitely had my attention. Hallelujah!

I was not entirely sure what to conclude from it all, and decided to ask God and Dad, "Should I write a book titled *Hallelujah?*" The next day, I received two unusual pieces of mail. The first was a brochure titled *The Word of Faith.* The caption on the cover read, "A Life and Legacy of Faith," and "Special Memorial Issue" was written across the bottom under a picture of a man clearly over the age of sixty-five. I checked the back to see if the brochure was addressed to me or if it was just a piece of junk mail that everyone in the neighborhood would have received. It was addressed to a man and woman in northeast Calgary on the other side of the city from where I live. Hmmmm.

The second piece of mail was a small advertisement from streetchurch.ca with a picture of a manger and a crown of thorns with light emanating from it. The caption across the top read "Jesus Christ came and died for you." It looked like it could have been cut out of something else, but I wasn't sure. Both caught my attention and left me wondering. Did these two pieces of mail have anything to do with my Dad and writing a book . . . or not?

I took a closer look. I opened the cover of *The Word of Faith*, and the first page, the first paragraph, the first sentence, was written by someone whose father had died! It said, "At 7:00 a.m. on September 19, 2010, my world stopped for just a moment as my father, Kenneth E. Hagin, went home to be with the Lord." These words had been written by a man whose father had passed over to Heaven one month before my dad. Well, this certainly confirmed to me that I was supposed to write a book, and again I found myself sitting there in the Grace of God, slightly stunned and very amazed. I said to God, "Well that seems very clear. Looks like the book is on! Hallelujah!"

The whole publication was a memorial to Pastor Hagin's life written by his family and friends. When I looked at the date of this man's passing over to Heaven, however, I realized I had misread it. It hadn't happened in 2010, but in 2003. *That's odd*, I thought. *A memorial issue in 2011 for a man who went home to be with God in 2003?* I checked the front cover and, to my astonishment, the date of publication was December 2003. I wondered, *How on earth did this memorial issue of The Word of Faith, published in 2003, and addressed to another couple on the other side of Calgary, wind up in my mailbox in September 2011?* A mystery, to be sure. Was it another small miracle?

Then another astonishing thing happened. Before all of his files had been lost, Michael had a background photo of Arianna on his BlackBerry screen. After looking at an email, he went back to the main screen, and the photo of Arianna was displayed. He quickly checked his video and photo files and realized everything had been restored. The dragonfly pictures were back. When Michael told me, I couldn't believe it. Michael asked one of the IT people at work what had happened and he said it was impossible and had no explanation. Had God restored them for us? Yet, another small miracle that had us in awe and wonder. Hallelujah!

On September 13, I thought, *I probably won't see dragonflies anymore.* Autumn was setting in and the weather growing colder. I felt a little disappointed about this as my dragonfly experience had seemed so sacred and miraculous over the past few weeks and I didn't want it to end. However, as I was walking up the sidewalk towards the front door of our house, after dropping Arianna off at school, something on the ground caught my eye. It just looked like a thin black stick, but for some reason, I stopped and took a closer look—a little nudge from the Holy Spirit, perhaps. It was a dragonfly. It wasn't moving, and I thought it might be dead. When I crouched down, I saw that it was on its feet, as if it had just landed or was ready to take off and fly. I waved my hand around it to see if it would move or fly away. Nothing but stillness. I was so happy to see a dragonfly, but I wondered what a dead dragonfly meant. Was it symbolic or just random? After a minute or two, I decided to move it. I picked it up gently by its wings and moved it to the soccer shoe shelf outside our front door (trust me, you don't want those soccer shoes, socks, and shin pads inside your house!).

That afternoon, I brought Arianna home from school and as I opened the front door to the house, she asked, "What's that?" Arianna had spotted the dragonfly on the ground that I had picked up earlier. I assumed a breeze had blown it off the shelf. As we looked at it, I suddenly saw its leg move. *Wow! It's alive!* I picked it up and marveled at it, thrilled to see it was still alive. But then I realized its wings were damaged, perhaps from my moving it. I didn't know if it would be able to fly. Arianna ran to grab my camera, and we took some pictures of it and then gently placed it down again. More wonder, more wonder-filled, more wonder-full.

That night, I Googled dragonflies to see if I could find anything that would help me make the connection that God or my dad seemed to be leading me to. The information I found shed some new light on my experience. In Japan, the dragonfly is associated with power, agility, victory, courage, strength, and happiness—also, rebirth, immortality, transformation, adaptation, and spiritual awakening. In China, dragonflies are associated with prosperity, harmony, and good luck. Harmony—that was my dad. Also, dragonflies can be a symbol of renewal after a great hardship or loss. Very relevant! Some Aboriginal cultures believe dragonflies can hold the souls of people who have died. The dragonfly tattoo quite often represents freedom and enlightenment. Well, this was a start and extremely interesting.

On the morning of September 14, I checked on the dragonfly that I had found the day before. Sadly, it seemed to be dead but I decided to keep an eye on it just in case. While writing in my God journal about this most recent dragonfly experience, it dawned on me: *Maybe God and Dad are trying to tell me that what we know to be dead is not dead, but still alive.* I felt that my dad was finding a way to confirm to me that he was still alive. Hallelujah!

During the time of my Dad's passing, I felt closer to God and closer to Heaven. I said a few times, I feel like I have stood at the portal of Heaven and experienced God's Grace streaming through. I think the majority of people who have a faith in God or a higher power, believe in Heaven and life after death—I had already embraced this belief as well in my journey with God. But somehow in that moment, Heaven seemed so real and so close, in a way that it never had before, even more than when Dad crossed over. My friend Grace doesn't say that her mother is dead but that she crossed over or became invisible. That was definitely my experience in the moment—Dad was there, alive and well in spirit . . . just not visible to my eye. Amazing Grace. Hallelujah!

I knew that this conclusion would not seem logical or rational to many who would read this. In the moment, it seemed irrational not to see this conclusion as rational. I had thought, at the time, I would only tell a few people this story because I believed that most people, even those of faith, who knew me to be a logical, intelligent person, would think I was crazy for speaking this way.

That afternoon, I decided to continue my online research of dragonfly symbolism. I read that dragonflies are iridescent and that their colors are a result of their ability to reflect and refract light. This ability makes them a somewhat mystical creature. They are inhabitants of two realms—they begin life in water, and move to the air with maturity. It is also thought that dragonflies are a reminder that we are light and can reflect light in powerful ways if we choose to.

I also found a blog written by someone who had an experience with dragonflies when a loved one passed and some of the readers' comments confirmed that other people had had similar experiences. Okay so I was not the first "Jesus Freak," as I fondly refer to myself at times, to think my dragonfly experiences were spiritual in nature, connecting me to God and Heaven, and my dad in Heaven. Hallelujah.

I also found this on a retail website called Sacred Cove:

Union of Matter and Spirit

Perhaps one of the most treasured gifts dragonfly brings to us is the ability to bridge the polarities of life. We are spiritual beings having a human experience. Yet, in the process of the challenging human experience we often forget our connection to spirit. Dragonfly asks us to dig deeper into the meaning of life, to see beneath the surface and connect to the rich realm of feeling within us. It is asking us to remember the ways of spirit. All life is a sacred gift, thus we cannot move through this life without an understanding of sacred spiritual truths to guide us and help us be all that we are meant to be. If we choose to live our lives on the surface, we will miss the vital growth and lessons meant for us. We have only to look around at the state of the world and our planet to realize we humans are failing to bring forth the gifts of spiritual law. If we long to create heaven on earth, then we must embrace both the mundane world of matter and the higher world of spirit. We will stay stuck in polarity if we choose one over the other. Dragonfly dances joyfully between both worlds, and shows us it can be done.

Overwhelmingly, the mass of website information depicted dragonflies as spiritually significant and uplifting. Hallelujah!

Then I came across *The Water Bug Story*, written by Doris Stickney:

> *Down below the surface of a quiet pond lived a little colony of water bugs. They were a happy colony, living far away from the sun. For many months they were very busy, scurrying over the soft mud on the bottom of the pond. They did notice that every once in a while one of their colony seemed to lose interest in going about with its friends. Clinging to the stem of a pond lily, it gradually moved out of sight and was seen no more.*
>
> *"Look!" said one of the water bugs to another, "One of our colony is climbing up the lily stalk. Where do you think she's going?" Up, up, up it slowly went . . . Even as they watched, the water bug disappeared from sight. Its friends waited and waited but it didn't return . . .*
>
> *"That's funny!" said one water bug to another . . . "Wasn't she happy here?" asked a second . . . "Where do you suppose she went?" wondered a third . . . No one had an answer. They were greatly puzzled.*
>
> *Finally one of the water bugs gathered its friends together. "I have an idea. The next one of us who climbs up the lily stalk must promise to come back and tell us where he or she went and why." "We promise," they said solemnly.*

One spring day not long after the very water bug who had suggested the plan found himself climbing up the lily stalk. Up, up, up he went. Before he knew what was happening, he had broken through the surface of the water and fallen into the broad and free lily pad above.

When he awoke, he looked about with surprise. He couldn't believe what he saw. A startling change had come over his old body. His movement revealed four silver wings and a long tail. Even as he struggled, he felt an impulse to move his wings . . . The warmth of the sun soon dried the moisture from his new body. He moved his wings again and suddenly found himself above the water.

He had become a dragonfly. Swooping and dipping in great curves, he flew through the air. He felt exhilarated in the new atmosphere.

By and by the new dragonfly landed happily on a lily pad to rest. Then it was that he chanced to look below to the bottom of the pond. Why, he was right above his old friends, the water bugs! There they were scurrying around, just as he had been doing some time before.

Then the dragonfly remembered the promise. Without thinking, the dragonfly darted down. Suddenly he hit the surface of the water and bounced away. Now that he was a dragonfly, he could no longer go into the water . . .

"I can't return!" he said in dismay. "At least I tried. But I can't keep my promise. Even if I could go back, not one of the water bugs would know me in my new body. I guess I'll just have to wait until they become dragonflies too. Then they'll understand what has happened to me, and where I went."

And the dragonfly winged off happily into its wonderful new world of sun and air . . .

Talk about powerfully compelling—this aligned with my experience! What a beautiful metaphor for transition and Heaven.

I read on a few websites that this story is frequently used to explain death to children. As I thought about this, I wondered, *Is my dad now explaining death to his child?* It sure seemed so. Amazing!

I put my search on hold to go pick up Arianna from school. As I crossed the street, a small red dragonfly took off flying and landed four feet away from me, on the road. I gently approached it but it flew further away, landed, and then took off again. I was astonished and happy, feeling Grace all around me. When I returned home, I saw the dragonfly I had found the day before, still sitting on the soccer shelf by the front door and was fairly certain it had died.

Resuming my dragonfly research, I clicked on the site of a spiritual life coach, named Nola, called Inspired Path. Her logo was the dragonfly. Nola's spiritual teacher, Jack, told *The Water Bug Story* in church every Easter, and when he passed over to Heaven, Nola began having profound dragonfly experiences. Also, when her father passed over, she once again had sacred dragonfly experiences, and still does to this day. As I read about this interesting woman, I felt I had some things in common with her and could completely relate to her stories. Another compelling moment of Grace. I was mesmerized and awed.

One of Dad's favorite hymns was *I'll Fly Away* (by Albert E. Brumley) which we sang at his memorial. When I Googled it, I realized it was written by the same man who had written *Turn Your Radio On.* I think Dad and Albert were on to something. The message of the song is very similar to the message of *The Water Bug Story*: we eventually transition to a place where we are set free and can fly away. "Some glad morning when this life is o'er, I'll fly away to a home on God's celestial shore . . . When I die, Hallelujah, by and by, I'll fly away. When the shadows of this life have gone, I'll fly away like a bird from prison bars has flown, I'll fly away."

The Internet seemed to be quite clear about the dragonfly and its symbolic meaning. My experience was powerful, spiritual, and shared by other people. Wow! I wasn't sure where this path

God had set me on would lead, but it sure seemed like it would be somewhere wonderful.

On September 20, I met my friend Grace for dinner. I took my journal with me and told her the whole story. I had written about these incidents in my journal whenever I had had time but did not spend much time looking back over them. As a wife and mother of four with three part-time jobs, at the beginning of the school year, I was pleased with myself for being able to find time to write at all. Upon full reflection, my entire experience over the past month, taken all at once, left no doubt in my mind—at least for the moment. I realized seven dragonflies in total had landed on me, including the one that landed on my God journal. And I had also had six notable interactions with dragonflies. As well, Michael's BlackBerry files had been restored, I had received the two pieces of spiritual mail, and the experiences with the wasp, the eagles, and the deer. At this point, it no longer seemed a question of logic, the evidence was almost over-powering—in a fantastic, formidable way!

I was reminded of the song *Tie a Yellow Ribbon,* by Tony Orlando. It's about a man being released from prison. He writes a letter to his sweetheart saying if you still want me, then "tie a yellow ribbon around the ole oak tree." And as he's about to get off the bus near his home, the man sees a hundred yellow ribbons around that old oak tree. I had asked God and Dad to send a dragonfly to land on me, and they sent many more than one. I felt as if there were a hundred yellow ribbons around my oak tree. It was perfectly clear to me now that Dad was in Heaven yet still with me—and God was leading me and I was not alone. When we feel God's love for us and a connection with Jesus and the Holy Spirit, we are able to break out of our own prisons and be truly freed by the love and Grace of God.

Months later, Arianna was asking me questions about the dragonflies and we were talking about the seven dragonfly landings and the six dragonfly incidents. She asked, "Wasn't Granddaddy seventy-six years old when he died?"

"Yes he was," I replied, intrigued by the connection she had just made. More intrigue and Amazing Grace!

At dinner, Grace Googled the name of the man to whom *The Word of Faith* publication was addressed and discovered that he had passed over to Heaven on August 6, 2008—the day before Grace's mom passed over or became invisible. This co-incidence seemed interesting. The obituary said that this man and his wife had lived in northeast Calgary all their lives until they moved to the southwest in retirement. I wondered where in the southwest, since this is where I live.

Grace also reminded me of the movie *Dragonfly* that was released in 2002. It had come to mind a few weeks ago. I thought I had seen it but I didn't remember it that well.

I mentioned it to Michael and he said, "Oh yeah, we saw that together in the movie theatre." I wanted to see the movie again and hoped I could find it on DVD or online. A few days later, I searched it on the PVR and there it was, scheduled to be on TV a week later. Another co-incidence. Another wow moment. Another God moment. Hallelujah!

Michael and I watched the movie together and many aspects of it resonated with me. Spoiler Alert! A married couple, both doctors, is pregnant with their first child, when the wife dies in a bus accident doing mission work in South America. In his grief, the husband starts to realize that his wife is sending him messages from the other side. Dragonflies are one of the ways she tries to communicate with him, in addition to flickering lights, dreams, and pictures drawn by former terminal child patients who had had near-death experiences. The messages are strong enough to lead the man to where her bus had crashed, and he finds his baby daughter being cared for by a South American tribe.

This movie embodies powerful spiritual themes of being led by the Spirit and communicating with loved ones in Heaven. The main character in the film is an atheist, so the messages he receives progressively freak him out as he begins to see the reality of what is happening to him. Everyone around him thinks he is delusional and "losing it," but he knows the truth of his own experience.

It is easy to become overwhelmed by our own or others' experiences with God and spirituality. Our spiritual journey can be compared to driving a car down the highway. We all think we are going the perfect speed. The guy who drives faster than us is a maniac and the guy who drives slower than us is a menace and "just doesn't get it." Similarly, in our individual spiritual journeys, someone up ahead might freak us out and seem crazy and someone behind might seem not to "get it."

I try to be careful about how I speak to people about spiritual issues when I don't know where they are in their own journeys. Part of the reason for this is that I don't want to be judged harshly but mostly I don't want to freak them out. A little freak-out can be interesting and challenging, but too much can be disconcerting and difficult to cope with.

I can only imagine what it must be like for God as He tries to connect with each of us in a way that we can handle. I think this is part of the reason why "fear not," is such a prevalent message from God. Often when someone encounters God or an angel in the Bible, God says, "Fear not," which I think translates to, "don't freak out." I was beginning to understand more fully, God's messages to "trust," and "fear not." We are all on our own journeys, and in the past year mine had become crazy interesting. Hallelujah!

I did a little more checking and found a few "coincidences." The couple whom the *Word of Faith* publication had been addressed to had been married for fifty-three years: the same as my mother and father. The service for this man's passing had been held on August 15, 2008. August 15, was the day that my dad's prostate cancer journey began when God told me, this is going to be bad. Also, this man had a surviving brother, as did my dad. I Googled the widow's name and found a link to a picture in the newspaper.

In June 2011, she had taken part in a local event called March for Jesus, which was organized by Street Church—the publisher of the other piece of mail. I found out her phone number in the white pages and left her a message. She called me back that afternoon. She wasn't a part of the Street Church ministry and said that a friend had invited her to the March for Jesus. She had no idea how I received her old mail in my mailbox. It was a mystery.

I decided to check into the other piece of God mail that was from Street Church. I checked the website and determined that Street Church is a radical Jesus ministry—this was both encouraging and daunting for me. I called and left a message, and a fellow called me back and told me about their street ministry—their goal is to feed, clothe, and preach to the homeless. They are a discipleship, evangelistic, outreach ministry. They meet Monday nights, pray for an hour, and then go out into the streets of Calgary and minister with the Word, giving out food, clothing, bibles, and God's encouragement.

I understood the *Word of Faith* publication because it connected very easily to my dad. However, the Street Church mail was a bit harder to interpret. For now, I believe that God is encouraging me to behave in a more radical way. Perhaps this book is my way of taking to the streets and "feeding" the spiritually hungry.

I wonder if there are small miracles all around us every day and we just don't see them. Do we have the ears to hear and the eyes to see? The experience of the past year has reinforced my belief that growing closer to God is like developing a sixth sense—you need to develop your ability to listen, hear, and discern. I think most Christians understand this to varying degrees, and we frequently talk about the biblical verse "Be still and know that I am God" (Psalms 46:10). This adventure with God has impacted me so strongly that I could almost *be still and be with God listening and knowing* all day long. Hallelujah!

One believer in a room full of non-believers could be compared to a sighted person in a room full of blind people. If the sighted person described what her vision looked like, the blind people would have difficulty believing what the person of vision could see, if they had been blind all of their lives. The blind people would all agree it was dark, and the sighted person would understand this because she shared that experience of darkness when she closed her eyes. But she would also know that her ability to see was powerful and real. This comparison gives me new insight into the lyrics from "Amazing Grace": "was blind but now I see." Hallelujah.

I saw a singer/songwriter, Naomi Striemer, telling her story on *Full Circle*. She talked about miracles and how we, and other people too, discount them. And we, people of faith, agnostics, and atheists alike, do this particularly in the name of rationality. While describing her shift from mainstream to Christian music, Naomi was working with Puff Daddy (a.k.a. Diddy, P.Diddy, Sean Combs) and a group of musicians and producers on a project. During this time she was approached by a chauffeur, who told her about a dream he had. In his dream, an angel came to him with a message for Naomi: the same thing would occur over and over if she stayed on the same career path—a great project or deal would come along, and just as it was about to take off, it would crumble and fall apart (sounds like a typical episode of *Touched By An Angel*).

Hearing about the chauffeur's dream was a powerful experience for her and Naomi had said to herself at the time, "God has talked to me here today." She said she had had an experience with God that she knew to be the truth, but that she knew she couldn't tell anyone about because no one would believe her. She believed people would try to explain the experience rationally, ". . . which is what usually happens when there is a miracle or something extraordinary," Naomi explained. "People say, 'there's a reason. We can reason this out. Let's be logical.'" How often do we do this? How often do we have a sense of the truth, given to us by God, but find ourselves wanting to discount it in the name of rationality and what is acceptable? Four or five hundred years ago, if you spoke against God or the church, you risked execution. But there has been a paradigm shift over the past few hundred years. Now, science is the new religion with tenets that need to be adhered to. If you go against what is deemed to be rational and scientific, you can be easily discounted. At least now you are not beheaded. Hallelujah! Even though lives are not on the line as they were prior to the 1700s, I think there is a need for another paradigm shift: both spiritual and scientific principles should be valued so they may work together. Not "either or" but rather, "both and . . ."

As the saying goes, "Why is it when you talk to God, you're praying, but when God talks to you, you're nuts?" Of course, an atheist might consider you nuts for praying as well. I've read the first few chapters of *The God Delusion*, written by devout atheist Richard Dawkins, and I've often said, "Either there is a God, or I am delusional." I do understand many of Dawkins's arguments because I grew up an agnostic and would have agreed back then with many of the things he says. However, my many experiences have taken me far beyond my agnostic roots. Hallelujah!

And like Farmer Hoggett, I realized that ideas that tickled and nagged and refused go away should not be ignored. I decided to write the book.

<u>Favorite Dad Memory</u>: When I was in elementary school, Dad had a book called *The Color Test*. It contained a set of twelve cards, and each card was a single solid color. The way you arranged the cards in order of color preference, indicated certain personality characteristics. It seemed surprisingly accurate, and Dad loved to test people. The test used both left-brain and right-brain thinking, another idea that Dad was intrigued by. I'm fairly certain that my interest in psychology was passed down from my grandmother, who was a family therapist, to my father to me.

Lesson: You can learn something by seeing it indirectly, as well as using your analytical skills. There are deeper meanings to be found and understood if you look a little more closely.

Chapter 15

Courage Over Vulnerability

Lord, I surrender my will to you and I ask
you to fill me with Your Holy Spirit
so I can be who you called me to be.

—GriefShare Prayer

I did not know what God planned to do with my manuscript, *Hallelujah*, but I felt that He would lead me. I was excited to tell the story. I became an enthusiastic writer and through the month of October, I began to feel an urgency to write more and more and devote more time to the project. I felt as if God had a deadline, but I didn't know what it was. Or perhaps God knew that I have always worked well with a deadline, which some might refer to as procrastination.

I marked the many anniversaries from my dad's walk with cancer:

August 15:	*Dad went to the ER; nephew's Birthday*
August 25:	*Dad went to ER; admitted to hospital*
September 11:	*Dad was released from the hospital*
September 23:	*911; Dad taken back to the hospital*

October 1:	*Grace-ful upswing in Dad's progress*
October 11:	*Thanks-giving in Dad's hospital room*
October 20:	*Dad said he wanted to go Home*
October 23:	*Dad went home to God*
October 27:	*Family funeral*
November 21:	*Dad's Memorial/Celebration of Life*

On Friday, October 21, I began preparing for the anniversary of the day Dad passed over to be with God. Since several family members had been away on October 10, my mom wanted to have Thanksgiving on October 23—the first year anniversary of my dad's passing.

In September, we had ordered a plaque and a tree to be planted at Edenbrook Gardens in Calgary as a memorial to my father and his life. When we were discussing the plaque, Michael suggested we use Dad's email sign-off: "Harmoniously, With Love, Dad." I suggested "Until We Meet Again." The family liked both suggestions and the plaque reads:

HARMONIOUSLY WITH LOVE
JOHN WATSON BENNETT
NOVEMBER 7, 1933-OCTOBER 23, 2010
UNTIL WE MEET AGAIN

Robert suggested we put musical notes in the top left corner. It was simple yet elegant—and to the point.

Mom had planned for us all to go out to the cemetery together on the anniversary of Dad's passing before Thanksgiving dinner, but the memorial plaque and tree were not going to be ready by that day, so the plan was cancelled. I felt that we should do something else, and thought about what I would like to do to mark the occasion. I prayed, and a song came to me—*Dona Nobis Pacem*.

I Googled it and discovered the words meant "Grant Us Peace." Perfect! I found the music and sang it while playing guitar, and I felt the peace of God in my heart. A few other pieces of music that I could sing with my family on Sunday came to mind. I also decided to write a letter to my dad. I thought it would be nice to write a letter that I could envision sending straight to Heaven, special delivery.

I thought it would be nice to create a sharing time with my family and so I sent out an email suggesting we each bring a song, poem, quote, letter, word, or scripture on Sunday that we felt related to Dad. Only Katherine responded to the email, and my mom had been barely lukewarm about the idea when I suggested it over the phone. I decided this might be the wrong approach for my family, so I let it go. I guess sharing didn't hold much appeal.

That same night though, I started to feel vulnerable about the email I had sent to my family. Then I had a sinking realization: if I couldn't send an email to my family without feeling exposed, how could I publish a book disclosing everything I had thought, felt, and experienced with regard to my dad since August 15, 2010? This growing realization of just how "out there" I would be started to make me really uneasy, and I wondered if I could really do it. *Am I thinking this through? Am I fooling myself?* Knowing how hard this could be for me, I began to feel a sadness I couldn't seem to shake.

When I sent the "It's a miracle" email out to my family and friends on October 4, 2010, I knew I was putting myself in a vulnerable position, but I was so elated at the time that I did not care. I was walking on God's sunshine. Usually, my internal editor would have stopped me from being so bold about sharing such thoughts and feelings.

Similarly, when I felt God encouraging me to dance to *Hallelujah* and speak at my dad's memorial, I was enthusiastic and excited. But the more I thought about it, the more I began to wrestle with the decision and wonder if it was the right thing to do. It reminded me of Jacob and his wrestling with God. A few days after the Memorial, I did feel overexposed. I was happy I had sung, spoken, and danced, but the feeling of putting myself out there was overwhelming. I realized that publishing this book, could create this same feeling, only times a thousand, or more! I thought, *Perhaps this is part of what it means to testify.*

In December 2010, I watched an episode of *Touched by An Angel* titled, "Psalm 151." Wynonna Judd plays the mother (Audrey) of a ten-year-old boy with a terminal disease. Audrey wrote part of a song when her son was born, and in his bucket list he wanted his mom to finish it. So she does. And she calls it, "Testify to Love." I love this song and I have played it frequently since then. I have often thought I would like to sing it in church because it reflects how I have felt all year about my experience with God. I have sung these lyrics many times in my kitchen: "As long as I shall live I will testify to love and be a witness in the silences when words are not enough. With every breath I take I'll give thanks to God above. For as long as I shall live, I will testify to love."

And yet, there I was, afraid to step out . . . and testify.

I had testified at Dad's memorial in a way that I hadn't before and I would be okay with this if I felt I had been fairly well received. But I wasn't. I said to Michael, "I don't think I would do well with persecution—and I'm pretty sure God knows that. I hope this is not part of His plan!"

On October 23, Michael and I decided we would go to church. We hadn't been in a while, and it seemed like a great thing to do on this anniversary. As we were walking in, the greeters handed me several pages stapled together with the bulletin. I glanced at them and realized they were sermon notes. Behold, the sermon was about answering the call and was titled "Searching for Callings." Well, this seemed relevant, to say the least. Then I looked through the bulletin and the order of service—it seemed as if the whole service was designed to get me back in touch with God's call for me. We sang *Change My Heart O God* which I love: "Change my heart oh God, make it ever true. Change my heart oh God, may I be like You. You are the potter, I am the clay. Mold me and make me. This is what I pray."

We also sang two other favorites of mine, *O God We Call* (From deep inside we yearn for You), and *Here I Am Lord.* "I, the Lord of sea and sky, I have heard My people cry. All who dwell in dark and sin, My hand will save. I who made the stars of night, I will make their darkness bright. Who will bear My light to them? Whom shall I send? Here I am Lord, Is it I Lord? I have heard You calling in the night. I will go Lord, if You lead me. I will hold Your people in my heart."

Again I felt like Jacob and thought, *Surely the presence of God is in this place* (which is also a hymn). God sure does know how to make a point! I had to ask myself, *Do I want to be led by feelings or by faith?* If God had hit me over the head with a bat, it couldn't have been any more effective than that church service. Of course, God does have a bat—a bat of Grace. This experience reminded me of the saying, "Batten down the hatches"—something sailors do when they are preparing for a storm in order to protect the lower decks of the ship. I felt God was telling me that there might be a storm, but He would protect me, and lift me up. I had been singing: asking God to change my heart, to mold me and make me, because I yearned for His love and Grace—and if God called me to bring light to the darkness, my answer was here I am. The theme of the sermon was how do we answer God's call? Do we even hear it? If we hear it, do we have the courage to act? Once again, I felt God had lifted me up out of the "mud and mire" and said, "Fear not, for I am with you, and I will protect you." It was shocking and it was inspiring, and it was profound. Hallelujah.

I was also reminded of Lisa Bevere's inspirational message in her book, *Lioness Arising: Wake Up and Change Your World*:

> *You are stunning. You were born for this moment. Don't be afraid of your strength, questions, or insight. Awaken, rise up, and dare to realize all you were created to be.*

I resolved to be fearless and let the chips fall where they may. And I would trust in God and His plan. Then I remembered how prominent the messages of "trust" and "fear not" (a.k.a. don't freak out) had been in January and February. God had been preparing me then.

Reassured that I needed to continue writing about my dad and the experiences of the last fourteen months, Michael and I had a family meeting with the kids that afternoon. I wanted to check in with them and talk about their grief and how everyone was feeling about Dad's passing a year ago. I read them the letter I had written, and sang "Dona Nobis Pacem."

We celebrated not the one year anniversary of my dad being gone but the one year anniversary of my dad being in Heaven with God. I was okay. And God was still with me. Hallelujah!

November 7, 2011, was Dad's birthday. And as I thought about that day, I realized that his birthday is probably not relevant to him anymore, even though it still is to us. Perhaps next year on October 23, I will wish Dad, a Happy Rebirth-day.

I know that Dad is happy in Heaven and that October 23, 2010 was most likely a glorious (glory-us) day for him. But I recognize, as Dad does I'm sure, that it is still a sad day for those left behind on earth. Perhaps it shouldn't be though. Fifteen years ago, a colleague of mine died, and left a wife and two young children behind. I said to another colleague, not knowing if she believed in God or not, "I'm happy for him that he has gone home, but it is heartbreaking for his wife and kids who will miss him so terribly." It turned out the colleague I was speaking to was married to a pastor, so she completely agreed with me.

In my twenties, I began saying, "I celebrate at funerals and cry at weddings." I believe that few people actually prepare for marriage and really have no idea what they are getting into. A funeral, on the other hand, marks a beautiful transition for the one who has passed. But for loved ones left behind, it can be the most painful and challenging experience of their lives. It can be made much softer through the knowledge of Heaven and God's Grace. This has been my experience this past year. Hallelujah!

October 21, 2011

Dear Dad,

It has been quite a year; I imagine for you too.

Is there a choir in Heaven that you have joined or are directing? The harmonies must be amazingly beautiful!

How are your mom and dad?

Is it lovely where you are—more lovely than any of us can imagine?
I hope the bliss of Heaven is more than you can stand; I hope you are in pure rapture!

Even though you have left your physical body on the earth, I know that you are still with us. Thanks for keeping in touch!

You must know how much I miss you and how much I wish you were still with us in body as well as in spirit. I know the rest of the family feels the same but you probably already know that ☺

Thank you for being "My Dad"—you did a fabulous job.
Thank you for all the great memories—they will sustain me in God's Grace.
Thank you for teaching me that Harmony, Grace, and Love are so important.
Thank you for watching over me, still, as you always did on earth. I still feel like you have my back.
Thank you for everything . . . 'til we meet again.

All my love,
Wendybear ☺

PS Say hi to God for me . . . Jesus too.
PPS Happy Rebirth-day!

I will, testify to love!
Hallelujah!

References

Arntz, W., Chasse, B., Vicente, M. *What the Bleep Do We Know: Discovering the Endless Possibilities for Altering Your Everyday Reality.* Health Communications Inc., 2007.

Bevere, Lisa. *Lioness Arising: Wake Up and Change Your World.* WaterBrook Press, 2010.

Berger, Susan. A. *The Five Ways We Grieve: Finding Your Personal Path to Healing After the Death of a Loved One.* Trumpeter, 2009.

Chopra, Deepak. *The Spontaneous Fulfillment of Desire.* Harmony; Division of Random House. 2003.

Dawkins, Richard. *The God Delusion.* Houghton Mifflin Co., 2006.

Dyer, Wayne. *Inspiration: Your Ultimate Calling.* Hay House, 2006.

Edward, John. *Infinite Quest: Develop Your Psychic Intuition to Take Charge of Your Life.* Sterling Ethos, 2010.

Kent, Carol. *Between a Rock and a Grace Place.* Zondervan Books, 2010.

Malarkey, Kevin & Alex. *The Boy Who Came Back from Heaven: A Remarkable Account of Miracles, Angels, and Life Beyond This World.* Tyndale, 2010.

Stickney, Doris. *Water Bugs and Dragonflies: Explaining Death to Children*. Pilgrim Press. 2004.

Vujicic, Nick. *Life Without Limits: Inspiration for a Ridiculously Good Life*. Waterbrook Press, 2012.

Walsch, Neale Donald. *Conversations with God: An Uncommon Dialogue*. pp. 77-78. Hampton Roads Publishing. 1995.

Websites

Heather Williams, Hallelujah, 2010.
http://www.youtube.com/watch?v=OX2uM0L3Y1A

Heather Williams, Hallelujah: Story Behind the Song. 2010.
http://www.youtube.com/watch?v=CG3n0htT-2Y

CANCER:

Inspire Health, 2010.
http://www.inspirehealth.ca/—
http://www.inspirehealth.ca/files/Integrated_Cancer_Care_Guide.pdf

Palliative Care, 2011.
http://www.avert.org/palliative-care.htm

Pub Med Health—Intestinal Obstruction, 2010.
http://www.ncbi.nlm.nih.gov/pubmedhealth/PMH0001306/

Canadian Virtual Hospice, 2010.
http://www.virtualhospice.ca/en_US/Main+Site+Navigation/Home/
Topics/Topics/Final+Days/When+Death+Is+Near.aspx

Adenocarcinoma of the Prostate Presenting as an Obstructing Renal
Mass. 2010.
http://www.springerlink.com/content/g282106u3q558817/

Creatinine, 2010.
http://en.wikipedia.org/wiki/Creatinine

Level of Care Designation: Resuscitation, Medical, Comfort, 2010.
http://www.albertahealthservices.ca/ps-1023351-103547-acp-gcd-order.pdf

DICTIONARY:

Dictionary Reference, Hallelujah, 2010.
http://dictionary.reference.com/browse/hallelujah

Free Dictionary, Hallelujah, 2010.
http://www.thefreedictionary.com/hallelujah

Merriam-Webser Dictionary, Hallelujah, 2010.
http://www.merriam-webster.com/dictionary/hallelujah

Merriam-Webster Dictionary, Hallelujah, Incredible, Miracle, 2010/2011.
http://www.merriam-webster.com/dictionary/hallelujah
http://www.merriam-webster.com/dictionary/incredible
http://www.merriam-webster.com/dictionary/miracle
http://www.en.wikipedia.org/wiki/Miracle

DRAGONFLIES:

The Waterbug Story. Healing Hearts for Bereaved Parents, 2011.
http://www.healingheart.net/stories/waterbug.html

Dragonfly Symbolism, 2011.
http://dragonflysymbolism.org/

Psychic Empath, 2011.
http://psychicempaths.blogspot.com/2008/10/dragonfly-symbolism.html

The Meaning of Dragonfly Symbolism, 2011.
http://theherbivorehippi.hubpages.com/hub/THE-MEANING-OF-THE-DRAGONFLY-SYMBOL

What Does a Dragonfly Tattoo Symbolize, 2011.
http://wiki.answers.com/Q/What_does_a_dragonfly_tattoo_symbolize#ixzz1XxnakGRe

Inspired Path, 2011. Nola Drazdoff.
http://www.inspiredpath.com

Sacred Cove, 2011. Union of Matter and Spirit.
http://www.sacredcove.com/news-updates/dragonfly-2/

LYRICS:

Heather Williams, Hallelujah, 2010.
http://www.youtube.com/watch?v=OX2uM0L3Y1A

Here I Am Lord, Hymn, 2011.
http://www.hymns.me.uk/here-i-am-lord-hymn.htm

Lyrics Mode, Change My Heart O God, 2011.
http://www.lyricsmode.com/lyrics/v/vineyard/change_my_heart_oh_god.html

Lyrics Mania, Turn Your Radio On, 2011.
http://www.lyricsmania.com/turn_your_radio_on_lyrics_ray_stevens.html

Tie a Yellow Ribbon, 2011.
http://www.lyricsmode.com/lyrics/t/tony_orlando/tie_a_yellow_ribbon.html

St Lyrics, Day By Day, 2011.
http://www.stlyrics.com/lyrics/godspell/daybyday.htm

Rainbow Connection, 2011.
http://www.stlyrics.com/songs/m/muppets9423/rainbowconnection
314602.html

Metrolyrics, Testify to Love, 2011.
http://www.metrolyrics.com/testify-to-love-lyrics-wynonna-judd.
html

Metrolyrics, Out of My Hands, 2011.
http://www.metrolyrics.com/out-of-my-hands-lyrics-jars-of-clay.html

Name that Hymn, I'll Fly Away, 2011.
http://www.namethathymn.com/hymn-lyrics-detective-forum/index.
php?a=vtopic&t=177

Lyrics 007, Let It Be, 2011.
www.lyrics007.com/Beatles%20Lyrics/Let%20It%20Be%20Lyrics.html

Oldie Lyrics, Till We Meet Again, 2011.
http://www.oldielyrics.com/lyrics/doris_day/till_we_meet_again.html

MISCELLANEOUS:

Eagle Spirit Ministry, 2011.
http://www.eaglespiritministry.com/works/ese.htm

Shamanism, 2011.
http://www.shamanicjourney.com/article/6031/eagle-power-animal-
symbol-of-spirit-vision-and-strength
http://www.shamanicjourney.com/article/6025/deer-power-animal-
symbol-of-gentleness-unconditional-love-and-kindness:

Babe—Movie Script. 2011
http://www.script-o-rama.com/movie_scripts/b/babe-script.html

Easter, 2011.
http://en.wikipedia.org/wiki/Easter

GriefShare. Grief recovery support groups, 2011.
http://www.griefshare.org/